Ion Idriess (1889—1979) is one of Australia's best-loved writers, with fifty-six books to his credit and millions of copies sold. When he returned from the First World War he wrote *The Desert Column*, about his experiences with the 5th Light Horse. *Prospecting for Gold* was his first major successful work; it immediately sold out and was reprinted constantly in the following years, along with *Lasseter's Last Ride*. Idriess spent much of his life travelling throughout Australia, collecting material for his true-life stories, including *Flynn of the Inland*, *The Red Chief* and *Nemarluk*. He was awarded the O.B.E. in 1968 for his contribution to Australian literature.

Tim Bowden is a Sydney broadcaster, journalist, radio and television documentary maker, oral historian and author. He was born in Hobart, Tasmania, August 2, 1937, and is married, with two children. He hosted the ABC-TV listener and viewer reaction program 'Backchat' from 1986 to June 1994. He has written 17 books including the best-seller *One Crowded Hour*. He has made several documentaries for ABC TV, and created the ABC's Social History Unit.

First published by ETT Imprint, Exile Bay 2020

ETT IMPRINT
PO Box R1906
Royal Exchange NSW 1225
Australia

ISBN 978-1-922384-98-0 (paper)
ISBN 978-1-922384-99-7 (ebook)
ISBN 978-1-922473-06-6 (limed)

Text designed by Hanna Gotlieb
Cover, edit and internal design by Tom Thompson

ION IDRIESS:

THE LAST
INTERVIEW

TIM BOWDEN

ETT IMPRINT

Exile Bay

PREFACE

In the winter of 1975 I was working in Sydney for the Australian Broadcasting Corporation. I had been working in its Talks Department since joining the staff in Launceston in 1963 in current affairs radio and television, with a stint as a foreign correspondent in Singapore and New York, and on returning to Sydney to start the evening radio current affairs PM in 1969. The following year I was seconded to television as an assistant producer to This Day Tonight the cheeky evening current affairs program, until the end of 1973, when there was a management palace coup and I was bumped back to radio which didn't worry me all that much.

I started to take an interest in longer-form radio documentaries, and in 1975, was intrigued to hear that the legendary outback traveller and prolific author Ion 'Jack' Idriess was alive and well and living in Mona Vale at the respectable age of 86. (As I write these words I reflect that I am now 83 myself.) In 1975 I was yet to turn 40, and decided to seek out Idriess to see if I could make a radio documentary drawing on his extraordinary life. Before I could meet Idriess I had to negotiate with his formidable daughter Wendy, who lived in a house high on the cliffs at Mona Vale above a small flat, occupied by her father.

As I drove towards their house, I was intrigued to see young men jumping off the sheer cliff tops, using the updraft from the stiff north-easterly with their winged gliders to spiral slowly up into the sky, eventually descending to the nearby Mona Vale beach for a controlled landing. I had not seen these gliders before.

Like the famous triple headed creature Cerberus, guarding the underworld (Idriess's modest flat) Wendy had taken over control of her father's affairs and book royalties, and she made it clear to me that I could do something with Ion Idriess for radio, but nothing else, and she would have to approve the planned documentary in any case. Neither I or the ABC could make any other use of that material without her express permission.

And so it was that I knocked on Idriess's door and was met by a diminutive bright-eyed old man wearing a woollen beanie and his slim form covered by an army-style greatcoat (the flat was quite cold) who seemed pleased to see me, and I began to set up my tape recorder and microphone on his kitchen table. On the small sink I noticed about 12 unwashed tumblers which seemed to have been there for some time. His favourite tipple, I discovered, was a mix of sweet sherry and milk, and I suppose he eventually must have had to wash some to keep going.

He was most happy to start talking about his adventurous life, but with some dismay I noted that his voice was a little piping wheezing effort which was barely audible to me, let alone the microphone. I placed the mike as close as I could to his mouth and hoped for the best. The omens for broadcasting seemed formidable. But he was anxious to get cracking, and we began with his first book *Madman's Island* (first published in 1927) where Jack Idriess and his companion Charlie were landed on Howick Island near Cape York Peninsular, where it was said there was a tin deposit to be exploited.

Idriess was not to know that Charlie, a World War I veteran, had been badly wounded in the stomach by shrapnel in the trenches and suffered from serious gastric troubles. The medicos had to keep open a permanent hole through to his stomach, through which chemicals had to be poured directly into him, via an instrument he called a 'scope'. Unhappily Charlie was so drunk the night before they sailed to Howick Island, he left behind not only his 'scope' but the chemicals needed to keep his digestive juices in balance.

I listened in awe as Idriess described how Charlie would be so distressed by his inability to service his stomach without his 'scope' that he would be literally go mad. At such times his stomach would swell up unbearably and writhing in agony he would literally go mad, roaming around the island with a .22 rifle shooting at anything he could see which included Idriess! To stay safe Jack would retreat to a rocky outcrop surrounded by mangroves which at high tide was separated from the island by a channel of water. He would conceal himself among the rocks during low water to avoid being shot.

Fortunately for Idriess, Charlie was eventually able to cleverly recreate his missing 'scope' and pour sea-water through the hole in his stomach wall which, over a period of some hours, would relieve the gas building up in his intestines and return him to some level of comfort and cause him to stop shooting his rifle at anything that moved, becoming, as Idriess said, 'me good mate again'. Apparently medicos of that era knew very little about how the digestive system operated, and with Charlie literally providing a window into a working stomach, doctors in Britain were keen to study him. But Charlie would have none of that.

And so *Madman's Island* a ripping yarn indeed, as were all Idriess's books written through his long and eventful life. I was fascinated, and we eventually talked on tape for some four hours, when I had to leave. (Mercifully I was not offered a sweet sherry and milk.)

As I went to leave, 'Jack' Idriess said to me: 'Tim, did you see those young men jumping off the cliffs with their gliders and riding the wind'. I said I had.

'Gee', he said, 'I'd really love to be able to do that'! And he really meant it.

Sadly no documentary was ever broadcast by the ABC, but I did archive the audio and transcript, which has been the genesis of Tom Thompson's excellent production and editing of this material forty-five years on.

It should be said that the chapter headings in this book, are taken from my questions to Idriess, and the only other interruption to his sprawling narrative are my questions seeking clarification over the fate of Lasseter's diaries and the lost reef of gold.

TIM BOWDEN

CONTENTS

The Bulletin

ABORIGINALITIES

The Boring Plant, Lightning Ridge, about 1910.
The Aboriginalities column masthead of the *Bulletin*.

1

Writing for the Bulletin

Well, writing paragraphs for the *Bulletin* was great training. It used to get me mad...I was a kid fossicking then, I'd carried my swag to Lightning Ridge (1909) and there my mate Tom Peel, he was a bonza chap, but he was of all the persons in the world he was a solicitor, and he'd been sent up there for his family's good..."For Sydney's good" - as he said, because he was always getting on the tank you see, and his people were social people down there and he was a terrible black sheep...Oh gees! he was a nice bloke, you couldn't imagine him being a black sheep, and by God he was lively when he had a few aboard - and some of the boys used to make whisky down below in the drives of the open mine, it was a little bit powerful. When a mob of them arrived it used to react in old Tom, my God he used to play up, but always good humoured and lively and as funny as anything he could be too, he was a great favourite in the Ridge.

And another one was old "Black Joe" - a bloody great big powerful old negro ex-boxer. He used to "Black-Joe" and talk like "Black-Joe" though his voice was like bloomin' thunder...they were my two mates. And me a bit of kid; it was a queer group but we used to get on wonderfully well together. That was the first (time) at Lightning Ridge. There was 1,500 men there, a lot of shearers had come there waiting for the next season to come to load up and go...you know, go back to sheep and other grub-steaking. Oh it was a wonderful life, Lightning Ridge; of course now it's all flattened out.

Old Tom Peel, he took quite a fancy to me and thought I could write, that's because of these *Bulletin* things[1], he said: "You can go a lot further than that, you'll be in author one of these days".

I laughed, like I imagined Little Audrey would laugh. Anyway, Tom kept at me and he kept at me and he got at my ego. I said: "Oh, well then! I'll write articles first and then I'll start writing books".

He says: "You? You couldn't write so and so".

Then he started scorning me sort of thing, which is exactly how a little freckled girl got me to write *The Desert Column*[2], every bloody word under fire. A man has got an awful powerful ego you know, even if he's only a bit of a Tom Thumb and worth about 30 bob a week, he's still got an ego if you can scratch it.

Well I kept on with the *Bulletin* thing, but they made you work hard, you had to consolidate every word to get a paragraph in there, by Jove. That was to stand me in good stead in years to come because I could edit my own books far enough to get them through a publisher, and then he'd put his own editor on - but the replies they used to send to our stuff, to everybody. It was a bushman's bible in those days and sent to the stations, all Australia wanted to get into the *Bulletin*, especially the *Aboriginalities* column and the society column and the short stories.

I started sending in my articles and they used to reply in their *Answers to Correspondents* column, "You're not an author's bootlace and you're never will be!"

And worse than that, oh, some of the replies... They was noted for it. It was a great fun to read – their answers to correspondence was a column in itself. I must've caused humour to countless thousands and thousands of readers all over Australia. Fancy those poor buggers getting this response to their bloody writing...They wrote shocking things, they'd make your toe-nails curl sometimes.

It was a great training as the years went by and you realised, because it got you so mad you'd write more. It was only a refusal but a valued thing; but by cripes, I used to say to old Tommy - he'd be lying there in his bunker at night time chuckling and smoking his dirty old pipe and laughing at me too, used to get me madder than hell. I'd turn around an abuse him and back to the pencil again, trying to tell him, "I've been working."

At last an acceptance came back from the *Sydney Mail*, the *Bulletin's* weekly magazine. By Jove it was a good one, I suppose this generation would know nothing about it, but that was a real good magazine. I wish it'd come out again and if they could get the same sort of stuff, I'll swear it would go very well. In those days Australia was only 5 million in population when I started writing, very different now; that's why you couldn't get an Australian book published: "Who the hell would read an Australian book?" we used to say, even the booksellers wouldn't take an Australian book, no-one would buy this in Australia, you had to be some bloody proud English aristocratic writer or something to get a word in that sort of business.

The Americans were real good if you could get stuff published over there. Some of our writers used to just live on occasional story they'd get from America, with the Bulletin; and then when *Smith's Weekly* came in we could some drumsticks, a bit of tucker now and again.

When I got an acceptance back, in great triumph, Old Tom and I looked over the cheque for Three guineas - it was 1910. I said, "The hell I'm satisfied! I'll get those so and so and so's who wrote me off!"

"No, you're not. You haven't got the guts to even write a book," he said. "What are you going to do? Just because he gets one tiny little article accepted in a magazine, you down your bloomin' tools. Down your pen, that's like downing your pick down the mine. Yeah, I knew you had no guts from the very start".

He used to make me just as mad and of course I kept on and after a while they printed many articles, short stories - the *Bulletin* used to publish me. They had me in a jubilee issue of theirs - *The Men who made the Bulletin*; of course that was a great triumph you know, because blokes in the back country - lots of blokes used to try to get in.

I would call Cowdrey at the *Bulletin*, I'd drop a request, I used about 20 names[3] you see, because you couldn't have only one name in it. And other blokes was the same, they had a number of names. But I've heard of a 'Gouger' and a 'Sea-Nomad' out in the back pub scouting for stories, so 'Gouger' I became. I suppose every other *Bulletin* writer was doing the same thing but all blokes think it bloody wonderful.

One day here in Sydney bookshop, it must have been after the war, I could see one of the counter blokes winked at me and one of the other counter blokes seemed to be having a losing argument with a customer who had a rather loud voice and was stressing his point and was saying,

"Idriess! there's no such name as Idriess!" he said, "If there is then he must be an Italian because there's no Australian writer called Idriess".

So they let him go on. He was a councillor.

"But he is a writer, he comes in here every day when he's in the city".

"Ah! You can't tell me a tale like that. I know better...I know my writers better than that".

And it amused me but I'm thinking: "I'd like to give you a smack across the chops you stupid git." He was a sydney solicitor...

Me? I'm staying down there, ask me anything about Cape York Peninsular and Torres Straits right to the Fly River in New Guinea. Oh, gees bloody bastards...

Cape York ceremonial dancers, photographed by Frank Hurley.

2

Madman's Island

An old tin prospector from Cape York Peninsular and me were in the West-Coast Hotel, Cooktown one day, when a Malay came in and said his schooner was wrecked on a place called Howick Island. He threw some black stones on the counter and said, "Here Jacky, are these any good?", and I picked them up and they were specimens of wolfram and tin and I said, "Yes, where did you get them?" He explained how when he was waiting there for someone to pick him up, he walked along the beach and the picked up these black stones, because he'd heard that tin was black, and he put them in a sarong and here he was.

So, me and this fossicker from one of the real savage rivers up the north, we hired a boat and we landed there and we found the little reef alright, but worked it out. We got a couple of tons of mixed wolfram and tin out of it before it cut right out. The biggest beacon on Howick Island was only 180 feet high, and then we were worn out.

Charlie, my cobber, had nine feet of his intestines taken out in London from one of those German shells - a war wound, and they patched him up at Guys Hospital. He had to report there every year - write how he was getting on, because he had instruments and things that went into a silver tube that burrowed down right inside, and he had to pour chemicals down this every day to flush out the gas. Well of course, he'd been so drunk in Cooktown he forgot all his gadgets and things....

So I thought: "Stone the bloody crows! Here am I on this barren little island with this bloke here". He got nuts and swelled up with gas and he went crazy, and the only weapons we had was his - he had a .22 pea-rifle and he chased me with it - poor devil went nutty.

Percy Lindsay's drawings for the 1938 edition of *Madman's Island* shows a young Idriess making a four-prong spear, and the evil Groper of Howick Island.

And each time this happened I'd jump across a big open space there where the waves and tide used to come and in I'd get among a heap of rocks and at high tide it was quite safe, nature would look after me; and then Charlie, he'd get rid of the gas business and then he'd be quite alright - a real good mate.

Anyway, you always carried a length of fencing wire it was so handy, and we used this wire for hooks for the galley. Charlie got a hook and he was busy there for a couple of days and I sat by wondering what the hell he was doing. He was twisting it into the shape of this tube thing that had to go into his insides. It was very, very strong to hold stream tin and he soldered this tin round and round in the shape of this wire. When he pulled the wire out he had made this winding sort of tube which he gradually poked down the silver tube in his inside so it went to good knows where, right away down in his innards...He was a grim-looking, tall, dark, sour-looking bloke, especially when the poor devil was filling up with gas, a narky old bloke he was then; real good mate otherwise though.

All we had to live on when the tucker gave out was fish - in the big mangrove swamp that was there, when the tide would come, fish of all sorts would come pouring in, and a lot of them would stop there when the tide went out; and we'd only just walk along over the mangrove roots and you could see these damned fish under your feet. They couldn't get away, they'd have to wait for the next tide, and there was plenty of tucker in there and they'd swim out to sea with full bellies - but both of us knew, being among the natives a lot, we could spear fish as well as they could. We made four-pronged fish spears from bits of wire and we could get them alright. Anyone else would starve because you couldn't see them with the reflection of the water, you wouldn't know where to look for them.

There were huge, big mud crabs - they were beauties, they had such powerful claws they used to burrow holes in the solid coral, imagine if they got hold of your claw. Well, I used to like them, they were our meat. We used to have real games of spying, "come and get me" with them, because you had to sneak from the back of the mangroves where they'd be sunning themselves out in front of the burrow waiting for the tide to come in with the small fish. You had to creep down, right at the back of the burrow and get right over them and then prong them with the spear; and the bugger now and then looked back, and if they saw you they'd dive for their burrows. It was a race between you and the old crab, it was who got to that burrow first; it was life and death believe me, and the crabs knew it too...by cripes, they knew.

It was frightfully monotonous, that used to be the worst thing, I used to sit up on top of this Howick peak waiting and waiting for some damned pearling lugger to come along and pick us up. And when poor old Charlie, he'd go nutty of course - he'd have me then. I'd have to leave my look-out and make a rush for this big pile of rocks for the tide to save me, otherwise he used to come after me with his damned little pea-rifle. He could never have grabbed me of course because this great huge mangrove forest. It covered many acres of ground. You'd cover the whole island in a ten minute walk going over every inch of it - except for this enormous mangrove forest. If I'd have to take to the forest, I'd have to hop up one of those mangrove trees with the damned tide and sharks and all sorts of great gropers rushing in with the tide; I would have had quite a merry time saving my bloody hide and being fish food.

One day I saw something odd while digging up on our mighty beach which was about 120 feet long. It was a piece of paper of all things in the world, so I lugged it up and this was the log of the *Seafoam* - the Malay's boat that had gone down, this was his log where he kept all the ship's accounts that you've got to have on your boat. I had an old pencil I always carried, as I used to scribble for the *Bulletin* then in the *Aboriginalties* column, and I sat up and thought: "Damned I'll write what's happening." A diary. I had to put in time, so I filled up his log of the *Seafoam* with this *Madman's Island* [4] thing, never thinking I'd ever have a book published. I knew I could write paragraphs but I never dreamt about a whole bloomin' book.

So out in our tiny little bay, which was only twice the size of this room here, walled in by the coral reef; this was our bay - "our harbour" we called it, hedged in with this coral reef from the open sea. Charlie took our billy-can and he lay sprawled out there and he made a funnel out of a jam tin. He put the funnel in the mouth of this tube and then he poured sea-water, instead of the bottle of chemicals he once had, poured that down his insides and gradually he got off this gas after about three or four hours. His belly went down and down and down. I used to sit there smoking on the beach, singing: "My God what a beautiful bait he'd make for a big fish", poor beggar.

Then he'd be after me with the rifle again when he got angry. He got on alright from then but he used to have to do it daily with the damned salt water treatment. We was there for seven months before a Japanese pearling boat came along and took me off. Charlie wouldn't go, he growled then: "What the hell has the world ever done for me? I'm not interested in this bloody world, you can go back to your bloody civilization".

So I said: "Right-o, you growly old cow".

I swam out to the Japanese, they met me, but it was a very dangerous place there so they stood off and sent a boat to pick me up. They was going to land me in Cooktown. So, I told the police the old bloke wouldn't come down. They went up for him, but he wouldn't leave for the police, he told them the same yarn: "What's the world done for me? To hell with the world!"

They had brought his stuff up. I said: "He mightn't come for you!"

When finally I got to Sydney, I had this damned thing with me - you see. I had a friend there, Alec Chisholm[5] the *Bulletin*'s naturalist. He'd heard about some quaint little hoppy-bird up in the York Peninsular beaches that he didn't recognise so, he could get in touch with me of course but he did through the *Bulletin*. He wrote: "When this mad, mad bloke..."

Why they called me "mad bloke" I don't know, but I was wandering all over the place. The queer things I used to see which were quite true and the quaint stories I'd hear from the natives, particularly the islanders, I'd put these into the *Bulletin* and every one of them was sheer fact. You see, down here in the city – they wouldn't believe them you know, they'd like to read them but... everything I put in there was fact. Anyway, when Alec went to the *Bulletin* he naturally knew all the pressmen, he was a pressman himself. He was one of the editors of the old *Daily Telegraph*.

He wrote me a letter asking me to come and see him: "Now come and tell me about this bird will you?". So when I went down to have a bit of a holiday here in the big smoke, I went to this *Telegraph* office and here was this great war-lord of literature - whatever you called them in those days, a real life bloomin' editor with his great big polished table, and

17

here was me... from "up in the Daintree". He used to call me "the Wild Man from Borneo".

I told him about his blasted bird and he said: "You ought to write a book."

I said: "I have written a book".

You know, I never really meant it like that at all.

He said: "Where is it?"

I said, "Here", and I pulled out this damned old scraggy thing you see here, the log of the *Seafoam*, and he got up: "Here, come with me". He picked up his hat, and I didn't know what he was going on or what he meant, but he grabbed me by the arm, and I followed him across the road to a place called Angus and Robertson's. He took me up the stairs and there was a great big bloke up there with big black whiskers (George Robertson)[6] which was very unusual in those days - with a very distrustful, rather humorous, suspicious look on his face - and an old lady which was old Bess (Rebecca Wiley) with a big grin. Aparently she was the boss of all the girls in my publishers.

So the bird-man with all his authority and pomp states: "Here, here's your great Australian novel."

It wasn't a novel, it was true stuff. It took me a long time to learn this that true stuff was just seen as fluff you see, and the old bloke just looked me and winked, looked me up and down and said: "Hmm".

"Bugger you!" I thought, "You bloody city shyster, so tell me about it."

So I had to tell him about it, and what Chisholm said - see if I can remember the exact words, he said: "Well, he's got a bloody powerful imagination anyway."

And I says: "It's all true!"

"Oh," he said. "How many years is it? Hundreds and hundreds since the first bard told <u>that</u> to the first bloody publisher".

I was staggered, I couldn't understand blokes down here not understanding how ordinary things happened, they used to happen all over the place in the bush and the coast in those days - all sorts of things like that. I went away and left the damned thing with him, I was to come back and he said: "I'll read this at home - for all the good it'll do me."

When I came back the next day with Chisholm, he questioned me about the thing again and he said to Chisholm: "Well, he has got a wonderful imagination - a wonderful bloody liar!" That made me a bit cranky

- you see, the cheek of it. I had a bit of an argument with him. He just stood there and grinned. He said: "It's so unusual. I might think about publishing it."

Chisholm said: "Yes, you're 'such and such' a fool if you don't, a bigger fool than even I thought you were," which was something to say for even an editor, to the one and only biggest publisher Australia had ever known.

To cut a long story short, Robertson said: "Well now, take this to where you're living…"

So I got a room out at Paddo. [7]

He said: "Well, write this out, taking care, but there's one thing; I'll only take it with romance. No book in Australia will ever sell without a woman interest - there's got to be a woman in it."

I said: "There wasn't a black gin within hundreds of miles".

He said: "I mean, a lovely white heroine, a nice young girl. Could you…could you? I don't imagine you would ever write a love story, but have a try. Say just enough so the publisher can at least say there is some feminine interest in it".

I said: "Struth! A woman would spoil the whole damned story".

He said: "No, it won't. There'll be no blasted story if you don't put a woman in it. Make a love scene somewhere".

I said: "Ah, stone the crows!".

What would old Charlie have thought of a white woman arriving on the island? I could just imagine it would be one long growl, and he'd spit, he wouldn't even consign to waste a word or two or a sentence over it.

Well they're standing me up very much to actually get the bloody thing published. I thought: "Christ, this is a funny experience…

"So I thought out a bloody love story for it at last, very much against my will, brought it in and he bloody-well accepted it. I thought: "Poor bugger! I do hope you don't lose on it". Mind you I was a bloody struggling writer you could say at that time, glad to get a five bob writing paragraphs up in the *Bulletin*, and here I was thinking, "Poor publisher, he's losing money on this…"

I learnt very different as the years went on. I learnt that publishers can look after themselves.

Anyway, I went back to Thursday Island then and out around some of the islands in the Torres Straits. It always fascinated me the people up there. A couple of years later I goes down, I'd heard the book was out but it'd done no good though. They wrote to me: "Sorry to say…", quite a nice letter, not what I thought he would have said; and I was real sorry for this poor publisher having a failed book. It was quite a big failure and he said: "We sold out the lot as remainders to Anthony Horderns."

I said: "Oh, poor devil."

He said, "They'll get rid of it. They'll get rid of it somehow, sell it for a few pence"…

"A few pence!" I imagined he must've lost a bloody fortune on it. So I sneaked into Anthony Horderns to at least have a look. I found the big book department and peeped in from the doorway, and the first thing that saw was a great long row about 4 feet high of ruddy *Madman's Island* - sixpence each! Oh, Christ, I could have cried for the poor publishers. Oh gee whiz! I really did feel awful as if I'd let him down you see…I haven't got a bloody sixpence out of them naturally.

I saw a rather nice-looking chap up there - Frank Fenton, he was a friend of mine for as long as he lived afterwards. Gees, he was a nice chap, he was the manager that was just building up Anthony Horderns book department, and I very timidly went over and made myself noticed…

"Oh this book," I said, "Oh, I'm so sorry but…"

"Oh it's alright, it's alright, they're going like hot-cakes"

I thought: "Hot-cakes at sixpence each, what must have old Blackbeard have lost on it? And what must this poor crowd lose buying this thing?"

The years went by and I wrote *Prospecting for Gold* [8], then *Lasseter's Last Ride* [9], six or seven successful books; so by this time the old Blackbeard (Robertson) said it was me who spoilt *Madman's Island* - it was me who insisted on that "girl stuff", that feminine romance go in - that's what stopped the book's success; "I'm really assured now it would have gone better leaving it as a castaway's book – a real man's book, a real he-man's brand sort of damned thing," he said.

"But I believe you were right strangely enough…" he said, "Just say the word and I'll cut out all about women in it and put it together exactly as you wrote it." Which he did and it's been selling ever since, right up until the take-over by Gordon Barton of our firm. Now that was *Madman's Island*.

3

Prospecting Cooktown

I was in Cooktown a year or two after Chilligoe. It would be 1911 or 1912 I suppose when I was first in Cooktown. It was all prospectors at the start, it was a tremendous rush and my God that was out in the back-blocks in those days. It really was a river of gold. There must have been a hundred thousand Chinese at least. When they made their fortune and shipped away back to China - of course money was in farthings in those days let alone pennies, and you could make a fortune quickly. And these Chinese made a fortune. They had to go back to the bloke who sent them out, pay him his dues, then they could live on their money for the rest of their life. They had to make room for others to come - you see. Bloody cunning the Chinese, well, they survived. They were really what we'd call educated men, when our own ancestors were carrying a spear and a club and were dressed in furs - they'd had plenty of time to get cunning, hadn't they?

I finally cleared away prospecting when I was very young and started then wandering, and in those days there was plenty of prospectors. I believed we'd always get out to the more unexplored county because there the big gold fields had been found and the only way to find a new field - gold or tin or wolfram - was to go right out in new country. Everyone who was a prospector used to get a few pack-horses and then you was quite independent. I got up to six or seven pack-horses and two riding horses, finally had a team, so I was quite independent of any man and could roam anywhere. I searched for several minerals, learnt about them but above all the country that I could expect them to be in; before I raced on fossicking in rock which had no chance with the minerals. That's one of the big secrets....

A Chinese Commission enters Cooktown in 1887.
Cooktown Aboriginals at the Barambah Settlement, 1911.

It took me about five years to learn that but I was in the bush and the wild places, until I was 42 - years before I come down to Sydney, and then I used to go away for six months every year. Sometimes I'd be away for a couple of years until I got absolutely caught up in a tangle, and what catches every man - you know, the women. You see some marvellous sort of thing, you can't resist them unfortunately, you find that out when it's too bloody late! You get cornered and yoked up like a poor old bullock drawing his wagon loaded with tons and tons of some huge cedar bloody tree and you're caught…

I haven't got any regrets really, except I wish I could live two lives - one where I was never married and always roaming, and the other if I could find a woman in which I could be boss-like, and if she was there...everything was wonderful as well - but I'd have to be flamin' boss when it comes to the opposite sex, not an oppressive boss but Boss! The poor old Man, he's troubled from the day he's born till they put him in his box isn't he?

Those early prospecting days up in the Gulf, I wrote a book *My Mate Dick* [10] about that period. He was a bonzer chap, Dick Welsh. He was a Cooktown boy and I used to go up with the boys there. They were all friends with the Aboriginal boys, a very plentiful population there, and especially across the bay; there was a big mission that was the toe-part of the peninsular and an interesting old missionary was in charge of it too.

In Cooktown, out towards the tin fields there was the tribes all the way out and right the way down to China Camp and right the way down into the south. Well those boys with Dick and all the other Cooktown boys used to go trapping and chasing things and especially their tracks. That's where I first learnt how to track an ant...Yes, you can track an ant, if you know how and you can track him right to his home, you can track a cricket...a tiniest little lizard, they leave tracks as plain as a bloody twenty-foot crocodile leaves...Well, in proportion - you know, but it's plain...

We'd track all sorts of interesting, funny little things in the wet sand and especially down by the Endeavour River where old Captain Cook anchored for a while. It's covered with millions and millions of tracks of things, these little Aboriginal boys would teach us...they knew what everything was in their tribal language - and of course there were all sorts of "eaties" under that wet sand, just scrap them up. They used to stand up with the toes and pull them up with their toes straight to their mouth. Under the bare sand all sort of things, especially where shellfish lived, they'd just crack the bloomin' shell with a stone and lift up another bit between their big toe. They'd have a regular feed when the tide went out, just standing there like that, these kids.

Of course, we'd used to follow suit and try it too, we used to eat the damned things like they did - some of them were bloody awful, and of course they used to warn us: "Him bad fella. Him bad fella" - that means you'll get a pain in the belly if you ate that scrawny bloody thing, which we was always scared of.

There was good bush tucker in the peninsular then, and plenty of wild turkey. It was scrub turkey, not the plain turkey because it was too jungle country, but the wild turkey that flopped down from the tree in front of you and said "goggle, goggle" - built huge mounds for a nest. They used to be wonderful those nests, there's be hundred of things in them, it'd be a natural incubator. If you dug down it would get hotter and hotter and real steam would come up, that was what was hatching the eggs you see, but you was liable if you dug with your hands, to grab a great big wriggly snake. That's where I first saw the most dangerous snake in Australia, the taipan. It was down there after these turkey's eggs you see. All sorts of things would run out of the mounds, things that I'd never seen at the time, as you pulled it down they'd run out and go for a tree, and up a tree. There was turkey and always plenty of wild ducks.

In every stream it was absolutely crowded with fish and I we learned from the native boys how to make fish-spears when you had nothing to catch him with. We'd get a stick and fire-harden it to a point enough to spear a fish with.

4

Life with the Aboriginals

How did I get on with the blacks in the bush in those days? Oh, very good. It all depended (on where I was) - like it did all over Australia. I've been from the east-coast to the west that's pretty near 3,000 miles, when the rest of the natives up there was wild it was, because the prospectors was looking for the wild country, a better chance for minerals - which it turned out to be too - and some tribes was up-guards and at 'em. You used to have a 12-foot spear through you with some tribes, but then a lot of tribes was only too glad to see you pass through their country to get the hell out of it!

If the Aboriginals had all stuck together it would have taken us many more years to have covered Australia, but every tribe was against the other. There might be one or two with an adjoining tribe that were friends but that only lasted a little while, and there'd be another language another few miles on. Some tribes would let you through, while others would sneak around trying to shove a shower of spears through your mosquito net at night time. We used to rig the mosquito net – they're bad up there in the season - and then when it got quite dark, sneak out way out and just leave the white net you see...It was much easier than going him, very seldom we used to go unless we heard them after our horses... We'd have to have hobble our horses. The hobbles we used to make because we'd be away from civilization for so long in the wet season. In the wet grass, the hobbles of our own leather would wear through so I had (made) two or three hobbles up there. I brought them down the last trip Sydney, still got them, show them to you afterwards if you're interested.

Meeting with an Aboriginal tribe during the search for Harold Lasseter;
Nemarluk in Fanny Bay gaol at the time of his interviews with Idriess.

Well, they'd sneak up and the horses could smell them and hate it. Oh they didn't like them at all and no wonder because they used to drive them away and then spear them - put them in the pot, or rather just chuck them on the coals you see. That was desperate for us, it was our transport gone, with hundreds miles in the wild bloody bush, you see.

We was always managing to lose our horses, but no shooting. I heard what our generation did to the natives out there, it was shooting in the streets and Christ it'd raise your hair on an end. It did a terrible lot of damage in other countries, they really think these stories are true. I've never seen one native shot in more than half a lifetime wandering in the bush, in the wild bush country.

I have fired at natives as I told you. Going up through those iron stone ranges they'd be waiting for us on the next ridge, smacking their bare backsides: "Come on you white bastards," flourishing their spears and this sort of thing. We'd fire at the rocks below their feet as we came on with our horses and they'd run down in the next valley and be waiting for us. A bit further on, a ridge over there, the same thing. We fired at the rocks again and that's how we got through some parts of the native's country, otherwise you'd have your horses speared or you'd get a bloody 12-foot spear through you. You'd see some of those things - it's a terrible death. And of course they used to - every now and again - get a white prospector, especially if he wasn't armed.

There was thousands of them then, there was game all over the place. It was a very easy country to live in but for natives it was just a paradise. They didn't want any gold and they didn't want us but there was so many of them; if we started shooting them, we wouldn't have settled this country for years and years to have come. Yet if they'd been One (nation)... but they never united, like many other native races uniting themselves into principalities and into whole nations; but not the Australian Aboriginal, there were 600-odd tribes.

A Northern Territory policeman with his dog, photographed by Idriess for *Man Tracks: With the Mounted Police in the Australian Wilds*, published in 1935.

5

A Man had his Freedom

A man had his freedom. The bush was big and wonderful, and he had one fascinating thing to entertain his mind, he'd go to bed at night no matter how tired, under the stars and the last bloody thing he'd be thinking: "If only I could find a nugget of gold as big as you", and some dream decidedly big when you think the size of a star. But that was it then, the other night he'd find a golden river and by Christ that was found, that was found in the Mandated Territory [11], and in that New Guinea rush they really shovelled up gold and shovelled it every day. I wasn't there at that one but a lot of my cobbers from Cooktown (were).

Cooktown was a regular place, Christ, they made a whole big fortune out of a tiny little bit of ground. Dick and I kept ourselves going, wandering about. When we got two old horses we were made, we'd walk and lead them and we could last for months - six months if we wanted to. We always had an old gun or a rifle with us, we could never afford a nice new Winchester. My first gun was a muzzle-loader, remember? That sounds a long time back, "a muzzler". Many a poor old wallaby I've shot for the pot - and turkey - with that old muzzle-loader.

As kids we learned to make our own powder and we'd get our own lead out of a specimen from the Broken Hill Proprietary Company – from any of the mines up there for that - melt the lead down and run it into our molten bullet casts.

Gunpowder - Charcoal and sulphur and saltpeter. We'd get the saltpeter from the butcher where he'd have the saltpeter in big casks, salting up the beef - to make it last in those days. We'd catch some of the saltpeter from his old casks, dirty stinking old stuff when that was wet; it was ours to dry and powder up fine, and we learnt not to be fools in mixing up our stuff with iron - because then it would blow up in our face when it got hot enough, see.

We used to make everything. The only thing that used to beat us was percussion caps, which we had to have, which we could buy then from our little bit of money. Dad used to give me sixpence per week if I'd play the blasted piano for half an hour of the day before running out into the hills with my friends after school hours. I was a wealthy kid...sixpence a week - that was money. Why for a penny I could buy eight bloody chocolate mice and eight of the great British bulls-eyes - lovely lollies, I don't see the kids with them today.

The most interesting one used to live up on top Mount Stuart all on his own - up there in the bloody wind and the pines and a big valley below with those beautiful great big cedar trees. I told (this) to some bloke in Sydney one time, he was a storeman that was going to close down, he'd worn out all his timber and he had quite a team of men: "Well I'll tell you there's a hell of a lot of cedar but you'll have to go to a new state". He said: "I'd go to bloody China if I could (get) some". So I told him about this valley, and he's still there, he's very old now, his sons run the mill but they got a hell of a lot of cedar. Anyway, they spoilt it, because it spoils this beautiful wonderful mysterious bloody valley; it's farms and God knows what not now. I'll rather it in it's wild state.

6

On Hermits Living in the Bush

Old George, "the old hermit" down at Mount Malloy, a tucker town way down in the flat country. Well Old George, he was supposed to be a nut but he wasn't a nut, and he could make all sorts of things. How he never poisoned himself I'll be buggered if I know, but he put me onto something which I've never found before. He took me away in the jungle - they call it a rain-forest I notice in books but it's pure jungle, that north Queensland jungle. He took me right in among the trees and there was about from six inches to a foot of sheer leaves always on the ground, rotting away - it's loam for many feet down...Oh, beautiful country to grow anything, and then he kicked away - with these great big feet, all knobs and bones: "I'll show you something Jack" - he took quite a fancy to me, poor old bloke. Well anyway, he took me way in this jungle.

He kicked the leaves aside and under there where the leaves had been a tiny bit higher was a mound where the leaves had been pushed right up - he kicked off all the stuff on top of him, apart from the big toe. He had hideous looking feet. I'll never forget them because we had to eat the thing that was under it. But it was lovely, and you know what it was as far as I can understand now, it was truffles - they're a great luxury in France I understand.

It was this great big rather mushroom- shaped sort of thing and I ate it and I've never eaten anything more delicious in all my life, just rooted down and here was this nest of these great big things, I can never find anyone else in Australia among all the bushies I knew who ever knew where they grow, you'd never know they was there. They grow under the top vegetation, and the only chance is if they happen to push the top and (if) anyone schools you enough to scratch that off, there are these big truffles.

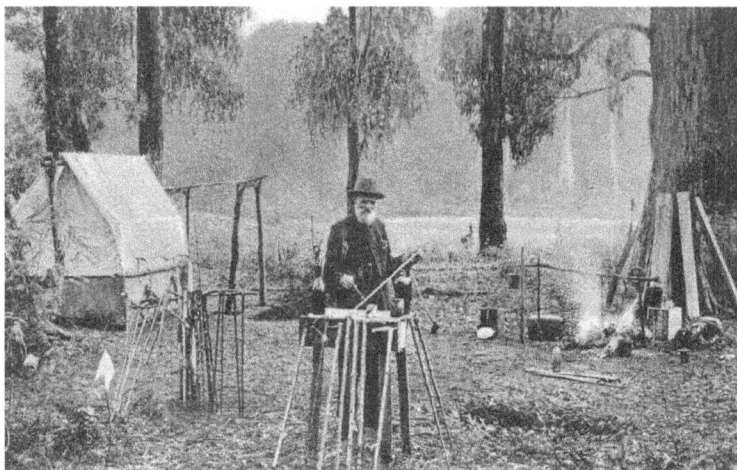

Hermit stick-maker, Queensland 1910.
Daniel Kimble lived as a hermit in Warnambool for forty years till his
death in 1904.

He could tell you all sorts of things like an Aboriginal and better than some Aborigines could tell you. All sorts of secrets about all sorts of crawly things and things that climb trees, that's what he would have seen - there's plenty of wild pigs up there… a wild boar chased me through those jungles one day and I nearly shit myself to tell you the truth. Christ, he could go that thing - and I couldn't find a tree that I could jump up… with this great big ruddy thing at my heels; didn't I tear through that jungle! And you know, you've got to sort of cut your way through and by Christ I got through…

These hermits, I think it was more a mental thing, they thought that they could learn things. Some of the time they really thought (that) if they sat out there at night time, especially on moonlight nights, they could learn things coming to them from the stars, and mind there might be something in it. As I grow older and older and think about all these waves, countless waves and pulsations and things they're finding in the air with these modern instruments; especially when they've made all these instruments to make this Sputnik and these flying machines. All sort of wonderful instruments they've found which they haven't told (us about). Each nation tries to keep as many secrets as they can, you can understand it. In this room there's countless pulsations and vibrations and all sorts of things going on, so what these old blokes thought, there might be something, they reckoned they could make their mind a dynamo or something or other that'd track what they wanted to learn, if they could get in touch with the vibrations, that it would react in the mind.

You know I used to think before I learnt of these things, it wonderful; these stars are hundreds of millions of miles away, yet my eyes can see them. I used to notice animals and that which can't see like we can see, some animals can only see a few yards, others can see a few miles.

The hermits reckoned they could learn many, many things before they died that they'd never learn in a town with a job and a wife and kids, and I can promise they were right there! The missus and kids would give them plenty to think about without listening to the voices of the stars, but there's me…anyway, my experience with those hermits was always flamin' interesting. I'd love to have it over again but I hope I wouldn't have to pay for my experience like I have with the first. I liked everything about them. Although I've got toe-nails I'm glad I don't get caught in the carpets.

Transport Lutzou – Bremen
18th May Cape Hellas 1915
                    Dardanelles

Evening. A shady line of cliffs,
the dim outline of ships, and the
faint Boom - oomm - oomm. Then
like bursting stars the shells hit
a distant hillside, here, there, over
there, here again, everywhere.
What intense excitement among us
of the Second Brigade as the big
transport came to an anchor. What
a roar of voices as an extra bright
flame crashed on the hillside. Then
dark night settled down, and the
bombardment ceased. .... Through
the night a great outburst of rifle
and machine gun fire broke forth
from the land. But most of us were
asleep, and heard it not. ....
Next morning we woke to the
Boom - Boom - Boom - oom - mm of
big guns, and going on deck we
saw a medley of war-ships,

The first page of Idriess's war-time diary, which became *The Desert Column: Leaves from a Diary of an Australian Trooper in Gallipoli, Sinai, and Palestine*, published in 1932.

7

Writing Books and Notebooks

I had to earn a few shillings to go out prospecting - looking for gold and there was few jobs. I used to unload the ships on Thursday Island to fill up the tucker bags, but there was too many men in the water. I couldn't get a decent job and with the wharfies union, there was too many men locally wanting a job. So the only damned thing I knew how to make a few bob was the pen instead of the pick. I concentrated on these paragraphs until I could write articles and get them accepted. By that time I took to the bush and for years and years I lived on minerals - tin and gold and opals, gems - even diamonds I had a go.

Few people in Australia know that there's diamonds in Australia but there was a very big field at Copeton within a few miles of Inverell. From there they sluiced millions of pounds worth of the hardest mechanical diamond in the world into the MacIntyre River. The men there were sluicing for alluvial-stream tin, but they cut the course of an old river where some extinct volcano had been somewhere and belched all his stuff in this old river, and in the sluice boxes was this retched hard quartz - always sparkling under the water flowing down from the river. It was always there when you had to stream down the sands out of the tin to get the heavy tin. With it being heavy it stopped in the sluice box the longest, but there was always these sparkling blasted quartz and the diggers used to curse them because to get the tin - then they had to tediously put it into dishes, swirl it around and pick out these quartz things and throw them away - they were throwing away diamonds! This went on for some years until someone woke up.

I was interested in everything I saw, there was so much to see in nature when you was wandering about, and different areas of country would grow different grasses, different timber and even different animals and different birds. Every swamp would have something different. There was something to be seen everywhere and you was travelling all the time, looking for gold all the time, there was so much of interest that used to happen. You'd be travelling with horses then in a month or two you might reach the Kimberley coast and there you might travel a thousand miles by catamaran - that meant that you'd have to watch the natives make them with a few logs and strong vines out of the adjoining coastline. A catamaran, that's a type of damned raft you bind together yourself. On you get and if you've got any sense you let the tides take you in the direction that you want to go. Mind, you've got to know just which way the tides and erratic currents go (otherwise) you go way out to sea, to Shanghai where old Marco Polo used to go.

Well, I was noticing these things all the time… I didn't write the first book until I was 42 [12] or something like that, by that time my mind was stored with all sorts of interesting things that fascinated me. It was the sort of things that the old hermits used to think if they sat up there in the moonlit nights, they'd learnt things mentally the same way that I used to pick up interesting things… Life was so wonderful from the earliest dawn to night time. No matter how tired a man was, it'd be a fascinating day and you'd fall asleep and life was just wonderful.

Wherever the men were, you used to form such comradeship. We'd always stick by a mate and that sort of thing, it was a wonderful comrade(ship). Some of my boyhood friends were still alive until each of us - fate and life took us our own way and that sort of thing, and I met some of them many years after when they heard about me (through my books) - where I was; and they came for many miles…Like, in Palestine for instance, and my old mates used to come (together) there until they were killed. We were still mates, and the only friendship that I've ever known was that deep bush friendship in those days and the friendship of men that have been in action together in the war - that was the same friendship, you never seem to break it… It loosens up after a few years in cities very often and fades away - it don't mean so much - but it's wonderful that the bond of friendship, of the old mateship in the bush and of the soldiers that have been in action together. I liked that....

The stories came out easily, like I can talk on for hours about these sorts of thing... in the bush anything interesting I'd stand there and watch it, to make sure it was accurate. If it was an insect hanging to a tree for instance, I'd wobble it about until I found all about it, like what was in the cocoon, and I'd wait there in a camp if I could and notice what flew out of it - out of a horrible cocoon there'd be an ugly-looking caterpillar thing. I'd bloody well wait there... until in time it was bound to recycle, I'd see it discarding it's bloody mound, and then the caterpillar growing into a butterfly... It used to fascinate me that sort of thing.

I'd write down (paragraphs) for the *Bulletin* and then perhaps in six months times I might come to some bush post office where I could send down a batch of hundreds of paragraphs, but I just had me notebook. Sometimes (I'd) write on jam-tin labels when I used to run short of paper... anything I could write on, it didn't matter as long as it's down. And then when I'd come back to Cooktown to headquarters I'd send them down to the *Bulletin*. They'd send me up quite a fat cheque you see, from all these hundreds of parcels I'd sent down. Well I kept that going. I used to hate it, it used to be a taskmaster sort of job for me, but I made myself do it like I made myself write down what was happening to do that war book (*The Desert Column*) and I got be naturally an expert at it. Well, I had all these notebooks, all these things with something particular put in there that I wouldn't have to send leaf after leaf...all sorts of subjects about all over Australia were in those papers. I could write another fifty books out those note-books there.

One time I went up to the Upper Nambucca, up the river from Coffs Harbour and there was quite a bit of gold there - enough to get me back to Queensland - and I met one of the old-time prospectors all on his own down by the river there... old worn out battler like he was and like I am now. He was always repairing these pipes, one of these handymen. There used to be a lot of them in the bush those days, could do anything with a hammer and a coal-chisel and all that sort of damned thing. Be on his damned old battery and he used to crush my stone. By the way my transport from this mountain right up the top of where I found my little bit of a patch, was a platform and elbow grease to get that blasted stone down from where the gold was to get it crushed. It was damned reef-gold you see, you've got to crush the damned thing. I cut down big trees, put a rope round my neck and I used to drag half a ton of this stone down this flamin' steep mountain with all its bumps, and then down to the battery; then climb up this flamin' great mountain and used to think it great, used to whistle…and I wish I could whistle now.

I got quite a few pars for the *Bulletin* out of that mountain, things I noticed – to keep my mind occupied doing the bloody camel and elephant act up and down that bloody mountain, and especially in the Torres Strait Islands with those fascinating races wherever they came from and their beliefs. Up there they've for countless years believed that men had come down from the stars. They used to reckon they'd sailed down like ships. When they saw our first ships…those ships and the sails they thought they was these super human beings. They reckoned that one of the big Islands in Torres Strait had got ancient fish traps… They taught us how to build these (fish traps) so that we'd never go hungry …these fish straps go for miles out to sea and three parts of the way of this great island (South Wellesley Island). All stone, cemented with coral lime in all compartments, a perfect maze… deep compartments for the big fish, smaller traps and this sort of thing, in the open sea and they're there to this day. They work down there for big fish to this day.

Now no white engineer has ever been able to that, if you go back in all the harbour waters…the storms are blowing to pieces with all our (wharfs)… but those great stone traps built, God knows how many years ago, are still standing there and doing their work. Now that's a bit of proof isn't it? They reckoned men from the skies come down in their flying ships to do that.

8

Drums of Mer

I wanted to get out to those islands and the Queensland government (banned travel) to Thursday Island and the adjoining islands. They banned that to any white people at all. They said they wanted to train the remainder of these strange island peoples to look after themselves. They were wonderful men. They used to form the divers for the ships in the old hells days - "the hell ships" they used to call them - and so the government stopped anyone going to those islands without some special permission from Thursday Island. They barred their wireless, they put their own officials there and they put a woman school teacher. She was great to the young girls. They saved it, those islands of Torres Strait; what was left of the natives to this day, when the islanders want to be modern like the white man, and they slow down the old traditions and are ashamed of them... the Queensland Aboriginal Department in the early days (did it), it was going strong when I first was there in 1926, and they've long since had their own fleet and the government...

The *Drums of Mer* [13] is based on pure fact, and those days of the white people, they're all historical. They were from the wreck of the *Charles Eaton*. [14] In *Drum of Mer* there was a wreck there and some of the islanders come on the wrecked people, knocked them on the head - they wanted their skulls to hang them around the neck of the great Au-Gud, that's the turtle-shell God.

They shaved most of their them and took them with them. Those kids in the book they were survivors from the *Charles Eaton*....People never believe (me), sometimes they half believe my stories but I tell you how you

The *Charles Eaton* was shipwrecked on August 15 1834.
The Charles Eaton Tomb is now at Botany Bay Cemetry.

can prove this one. Lots of people say: "Well, it's very interesting reading a strange book *Drums of Mer,* but of course he must of coloured that in..." Well, bugger it, the proof is right in your own cemetery here in Sydney - old Botany cemetery, there's some of the skulls of the *Charles Eaton* in our own cemetery. There's a placard on it describing the (Colonial) government's *Isabella* went up and rescued them from the great Au-Gud there's...right in your own cemetery.[15]

Not long afterwards it was rumoured through traders that there was captives up there, they were (from) the *Charles Eaton*, and the *Isabella* schooner went up there and landed on these different islands, they found the Au-gud - it was a gigantic tortoiseshell (mask), I don't remember if it's mentioned on the placard out here in Botany...It's a beautiful thing, savage bloody hide of a thing but out of tortoiseshell so it would be worth a lot of money even in those days. This schooner found their skulls necklaced around the great Au-gud and they brought those necklaces and other relics down and buried them.

Wondering what had happened about the *Isabella* - vague rumours, legends of those times. None of the whites of those days believed it you see, but by some bloody fluke I read in some old government gazette that they buried them out at Bunnerong. I went all through those cemeteries and there's a great big stone plaque laying over, fallen over with age, but it's got a copper plate on it and there's the whole story of the tragic wreck of the *Charles Eaton*... now don't you reckon that should be verifying a fact right enough?

Well, through the wandering missionary (Rev. William Macfarlane[16]) - it's most unusual for a prospector and a missionary to chum-up together, but he was a writer like me and his father was the first man of the missionaries to come through from New Guinea to the natives there. In those days, their way was to convert the natives they come across and where they landed was the tree of skulls. Sibai Island is right against New Guinea. The Tugeri (warriors from the Marind-Anim tribe) would come down... Oh, for thousands of years I suppose, and try and take a few of the Torres Strait heads, but on this low-lying island they had their tree up top with a big house where they used to jump up you see, and say, "Come up you bastard and get us!'. They'd send their arrows down and the New Guinea men would send their arrows up and there was a disadvantage, they lasted all those years, and all the heads of the Sibai men was on a big bushy tree down there, and here they had all the skulls on it.

Unfortunately MacFarlane's dad (Rev Samuel Macfarlane[17]) came along and put the fire-stick to their men's house and defence house, and their idol, to them to teach the savages - you know, "our way", our bloody way. They couldn't burn the tree of skulls but they got down as many (skulls) as they could and buried them.

When I got there it was covered - not with tortoise but big shells - the nearest approach to represent it by this time, and just way up top there was three dirty, grey-looking, pathetic-looking things falling to pieces, it was all that was left of the many skulls.

Oh, with MacFarlane, his was a lifetime study by that time - and he used liked to write for the same magazines - the *Mail* magazine, and he used to write paragraphs for the *Bulletin* from Thursday Island. That's how I got to know him from when I come down to Sydney . I used to like his articles - his very rare articles on the Torres Strait Islands, that's how I'd made up my mind I must go and see the bloke. So when I went up I called on him we got (on) together straight away. And with him and his mission ketch *Herald* I've landed in every island in Torres Strait, they're only small and there's not so many of them. The islands between the tip of Cape York Peninsular and Papua - at the end of Papua, just those islands between, but they have the most fascinating history... far more than any others of the many islands I've visited you see.

Well, with Macfarlane and the *Herald* out there, we camped on island after island where he had his men and he'd organised to hold hands to make peace and that sort of thing , The old native priests got a real priest-hood there, all sorts of laws and by cripes, they were serving masters at mesmerism, and what that's other close allied thing, hypnotism. It was in chapters of the first (draft) *Drums of Mer* and that's what I've seen them do; people lie down for them and all sort of messy-looking things they used to draw out of them; these old blokes - before my eyes, unless they had me hypnotised. Anyway, they'd get up and were bloomin' well cured.

But our reader at Angus and Robertson at that time said: "You daren't publish this, this is ridiculous, it'd even make Angus and Robertson the laughing stock all over Australia". So the most interesting chapters of the lot (were to be cut) and finally I got narked, I took them back and I burnt them. I wish I never bloody well had. The stuff there, if I could only remember all that stuff.

We used to sit down - MacFarlane – and the old Zogo-le with the old remnants around us in the Zogo house and I'd ask questions, and I'd write (down) the answers. MacFarlane would ask of these old hands who'd been there all their lifetime and knew all the stories of their ancestors. That's where he got the stories from the leaders, of the men up in the sky who'd come down in their sailing ships to teach them how to make the great fish traps and how to make life easier and what trees to grow on the islands... You could have spent months listening (about) Kebisu and his bloody warriors, he defended the whole bloody lot of them. We'd sit down night after night and I'd write down their answers see. *Drums of Mer* was all questions, and I got to learn a bit with the questions I asked, and they gave me details.

In one way they had the very strict laws but this was all for the tribe, for the combined safety of the tribe, where they had enemies everywhere. And if anyone broke a law that meant it was a start for someone else to be game enough to do if they wanted to, whereas, they reckoned if they were all stuck together from birth to death it'd be only by the greatest bad luck that they could be broken, and that's how they existed in different tribes. Some of those tribes in the Torres Straits they'd join together. If anyone else came they could fight with one another if they wanted to, but they didn't much want (to fight) among themselves because they had plenty to do, looking after their own trees and vegetables. They grew all sort of native vegetables, these men in the sky taught them, they reckon. A lot of them came from New Guinea, a lot of their different yams and that sort of thing, as it's tremendous the vegetation in New Guinea. They would have been told where to get foods and either fight or trade with the New Guinea people, that was the usual way in those days.

I can tell you a joke now about that Dance of Death. Now, I've seen in the press: "Idriess must have gone drawn the long bow, he's coloured it a little bit... drawn the long bow here surely." With a condemned warrior, they knock him on the head in such a way the blood spurts out and he

keeps on running with the blood spurting out. To me it was so simple…
I seen my own Dad killing the Sunday bloody rooster for the pot. Often
if you hit him with the axe just between these two bones, you can feel
those bones there, that rooster will run around the yard. Well that's
exactly the same (on Mer). Strangely enough only a few years later I
read something about a condemned criminal in China - someone
reporting it, and when the axe-man chopped his head off he jumped up
to the astonishment of the crowd, running round and round with blood
spurting - exactly (like) the Dance of Death. Well, anyway that was
first chapter (in *Drums of Mer*) as far as my faulty memory goes and I'm
sure it was.

This book was very popular. All my books (were) by this time, they sell
out at the first editions. They had to before Christmas in those days, otherwise I wouldn't have had the money for a bloody crust, books had to sell.

Well, by the way they grew up to be - me and (E.V.) Timm's [18] (together
sold) 16,000 and 20, 000 of the first editions, and to sell out before
Christmas, and now they tell me if they sell 3,000 copies - what on earth
has happened to the writers? If they sell 3,000 of the first edition, they
reckon it's wonderful. I can't understand it, I thought long before now
we would have had Australian authors sell 30,000 or 40,000 for a
Christmas edition, I can't understand it.

Well, at least a score of fan-mail came from women and maybe what a
breath of relief - getting rid of the old man and the kids, and they read this
awful blood thirsty chapter and they all said they were sick in the bath…
Do you know, I have a hysterical laugh at every one of them, I thoroughly
enjoy those bloody letters. What man would laugh at a poor woman being
sick in the bath?

We'd sit down wherever he had the chance with the native councillors,
these old rogues, the blood-thirsty old priest-hood, they brought them
into their (new) priest-hood. They were the native councillors and
they were responsible for keeping order in their island, and for getting all
they could out of the government. The government would help them in
every way, they must keep their certain order, no more head-hunting, not
unless they were attacked and that sort of thing.

And each island was treated the same way so they had very important
councillors and as they were already the feared priesthood of the locals

there, they were obeyed and it suited the old blokes. One of the old blokes - when they got to know me - he says: "Look it was great Jack, we hate - to put it in my language - we hate to see the young fellas all going the white man's way and thinking more of the white man's God and the white man's beliefs. We must now realise that but it makes our hearts sore to see…" he said, "Now look at this, I fear now will I ever be able to use it." He showed me a dirty-looking dried up pea, a fair size....

"I might never be able to use this… I'm trying hard to use it before it's too late, but I find it more and more difficult to get in touch with. This is for my nephew in New Guinea - this is my enemy's tongue..."

Sun-dried, his enemy's tongue.

"He's got to swallow this and this will give him his strength as a great fighting man, a great warrior. He's got to swallow this and his enemy's spirit will come out and make him a strong powerful savage warrior. But I can't get at him and he's going very strong, he's going to the white man's school and he's only sixteen - I'm afraid he's going all out to be a white man, and he's inclined to laugh at the old men's ways and that sort of thing".

There's this horrible-looking bloody thing, and he was one of the leading councillors of the church - of our church. He was one of the main councillors on this island you see, keeping the rest of the wild country. He had to take it, to take certain vows from the Zogo-le when he took it and another Zogo had to witness, then he was one of them, he could have the courage to be as big a man as Zogo-le. If he was good enough, he's grow up to be a real man sort of business.

Macfarlane had them all under his thumb like that, he would never have managed but for some clever idea like that you see, and of course he was in close touch with the Aborigines Department on Thursday Island and anything that he thought that the whites could do for them - the Aborigines Department would send out to Thursday Island for him and he'd hand it out you see, always keeping the strong hand - in the hand.

Torres Strait people were very nice people. A laughing people, brown people, very intelligent, they weren't very tall but they were very broad, that was because - women and all - they were such wonderful swimmers. They lived in these islands, they lived practically in the water, they could swim under water for an amazing length of time, and their life was as much in the water as on the land. The main defence was absolutely a navy in the smallest island of all and without any water on it, that was Warrior Island. And there was a wonderful chief called Kebisu (from Yama Island) and he had built huge canoes with sails of coconut palm, treated in a certain way they could stand almost the biggest storms, and these were huge and would take 100 warriors each. They had bows that I could lift the bow string, they used to remind me exactly of the stories of boyhood days of the longbow men of the yeomanry of England - they're huge longbows that used to go to war with, and were a backbone (for) British armies of those days.

I could lift the bow back, they were very powerful. They used to sail up and down that Strait. New Guinea of course had far the greatest number of warriors. They were supposed to have had a couple of million men when our first whites entered New Guinea. If they'd come in raiding it'd be Kebisu's men to be the first to meet them, and they fired a rear-guard action. Everyone would have to fight from their islands, but Kebisu could manoeuvre his fleet anywhere, and he was a terror of any enemy of bigger numbers because he could attack from anywhere - the rear or anywhere and with these great canoes of his. They were wonderful sailors, and the Warrior Island men were wonderful warriors.

One of the English war ships, *HMS Baselisk* came and anchored by that island, and he had just in case he was attacked by Kebisu's warriors, his gun loaded with grey-shot and chain-shot - that was a big chain as you imagine. Say, a twenty foot length of chain is fired out of a canon, it unwinds in the air and whirls round and round and round. It'd cut through a tribe, it's bloody worse than our shrapnel of these modern days. You imagine the chain the size of this room whirl round and round a mob of natives. Stone the crows, a mob of whites couldn't stand up against grey-shot.

These chaps did have designs on this cheeky English captain (Captain John Moresby), and Kebisu says he wasn't scared of these men with the spirits, they thought anything worthwhile was like the ships they reck-oned came down from the sky. They call us, the white people, the Migiloo, that's spirit people - see they'd come down from the sky for a period here to learn what things were doing on earth, then they'd fly back as ships of spirit people back to the skies. They had marvellous sort of beliefs like that, it fascinated me.

So *Drums of Mer* all came from the old Zogo-le, night after night answering my questions with MacFarlane. I would never have heard of those things you know, never have heard of all the things that's in the book, and that's only fragments, like the notebooks there. I could write a couple more books about that same island, and from those there.

Murray Island ceremonial dancers, Mer 1908.

Lismore 1890s when Idriess was there.
Chinese gold-miners head for the diggings on top of a Cobb
& Co coach.

9

Early days in the Central West

When I was a kid in knickerbockers, Dad was a Sheriff's Officer and Inspector of Mines, well that meant he'd be moved from township to township as it grew in importance, and with many towns we visited he'd have to go out in the bush where there were scattered mines all over the district. He was stationed in NSW and he had to inspect the mines for the prospectors with the Government Mining Department, and there was all sorts of outside mining work.

I'd often travel with him, especially in Christmas holidays in the sulky and there was always plentiful blacks then in NSW. I didn't meet the wild blacks until I got up in the north of Queensland, but Dad liked the Aboriginals and they used to catch tobacco from him and all sorts of little favours, and in every town we was chummy with the outside blacks. Well I was only actually a baby when I first saw them, and when we were stationed at Lismore. Lismore then wasn't the lovely city it is now but it was just a tiny country township where you'd see a man in corduroys just walking along down the street with his horse kicking up a bit of dust from his heels, that sort of thing, a few timber cutters having a drink or two... it was just a township. We lived three miles out of Lismore at a place called Booerie Creek and down at the river, at the bottom of our huge paddock, was the local tribe of blacks. They were very sophisticated even in those days and they'd go into town on Saturday, and among them was some of the black gins, they were very knowledgeable ladies indeed. Well they'd come out screaming mad, blithered in the night time and fight their way back - with the black men.

So on Monday they'd come crawling up and they knew when Dad would go into town - three miles to drive there - Mum would be home and she was very frightened of them, she could never get used to them. These old girls knew they could bully mum, and they used to catch nearly all the tucker that'd be in the house sometimes before she could shoo them away with all sorts of veiled threats and that sort of thing. That's when I got really to know them, they were just human beings like us, although very different to us and I took an interest in them, especially the piccaninnies from a very tender age. And every place we went - except Broken Hill which was a good many years later - there was always a tribe of blacks camped down at the creek or at the river in whatever township Dad was stationed. So from a very tender age I began to take an interest in them.

I left home, somewhere about 18 and 19 and I carried my swag...the opal fields at Lightning Ridge had been found then so I carried my swag there. I've never forgotten meeting the Cobb & Co coach in that trip coming along, it's hard to think that even in a living man's time that all our transport was done by horses and the travel by Cobb & Co's coach...

I was going along this track from Walgett and all I could here was the crows that was following me along the edge of the timber and the big station Dungaleer Station. There was the crows and the bright sunshine and the cockatoos was screeching at me as you went past and life was wonderful. I was dreaming of finding a big opal mine and all that sort of thing that man dreams of all through his life, more or less anyway, and in the distance I saw a big cloud of dust coming. I watched for a while and then I could hear shouting and seeing far in the distance coming along - and a bloomin' banjo playing and the horn blowing - they used to have a bullock's horn and blow "here comes the coach!" You could hear it for a mile, and so it rapidly drew closer and closer and there was the Cobb & Co's coach. They had six horses and coming hell-for-leather - for at Walgett you see they changed the horses and it was packed; blokes sitting up on top, and heads leaning out of the bloomin' window and there they was all singing; and as they approached me the driver blew his horn again and waved his whip, and I waved my hand and the blokes gave a great "Hoorah!": and that swine nearly smothered me in their blasted dust and I yelled and they yelled, and away they'd gone...

Cobb & Co… in my bloody day, every bush road had Cobb & Co's coaches on, that's the only way you could travel unless you had your own horse and your buggy - and that's something in my lifetime. Since then we've gone to the moon, it's bloody wonderful when you think of it... the motor car, internal combustion engine, they put even the horses out of business at last, and the old bullocks put them out of business. I'm glad they did because the horses and the big heavy transport then it'd be very heavy, life was hard when I was a kid. Poor devils used to toil themselves to death of course.

Edward Milne at the site of the grave of Yuranigh (died 1850) at Gamboola, near Molong in 1912. It is the only example of a grave with both Aboriginal and European monuments

Aboriginal hunting party in the Kimberleys as photographed by Idriess.
Norman Tindale with Aboriginals at Rockshelter, Bathurst Head, Eastern
Cape York Peninsular 1927.

1 0

Aboriginals of Cape York and the Kimberleys

There was still some mobs right at the top of Cape York Peninsular, par-ticularly the west-coast where sandalwood cutters used to have to go down and they had to bribe the tribes down there. They were what we call "cheeky fella." They'd like to have a go at the white man sort of busi-ness you see. There were wild ones down there and in the east-coast now and again there were pretty cheeky ones, but they'd got fairly used to the whites; for a prospector going up and finding half a dozen little gold fields up there you see.

When I went to the Kimberleys there were plenty of wild ones there - tribes of them, and in parts of the Territory they were still wild, plenty of parts of the Territory, because the Territory was just a huge, big almost unoccupied country then. I think Victoria Downs was one of the few stations there, it was as big as Belgium they used to say in my day - that one station, Christ!

Almost ninety percent of those photos in the books I took myself. I went up 3,000 miles with a police patrol in the Kimberleys.[19] Of course I had to get permission from the chief of the Police Department in Perth, and they bought me a camera with a Zeiss Icon lens which is a wonder-ful lens even today. Reviewers said, these copies should be sent to some photographic government department in Paris apparently well-known, so they must've been good because I knew nothing about photography, they were just fluke ones.

One day I was way out in the back-blocks and was camping with the only man there - a selector. He'd brought his baby there, brought her by camel all through this country and made a selection of this wild beautiful little spot by a place called the Sale River - beautiful little place. I was camping with him for a time until the patrol came. They'd gone right to the coast so I was going to wait for them there to come back. We just sitting there, smoking a cigarette, watching all the little birds running across the water-lily leaves when I heard a tiny little patter-patter and here was a young gin. I didn't move, and of course you know, as long as you don't move, even wild trained men could pass you by and not see you...The aeroplanes can't see you unless you move you know. Anyway I stood still...Being a gentleman I should have gone but I didn't, she come along... A lovely girl in front of me and she was a real woman. She'd never seen a bloody white woman until this young selector brought his wife along, but she stood by that pool like another of the young girls in North Queensland and washed the same way, and she tucked her hair over her head and back. She did all the showing, a little of everything and she looked damned good; young gins are very slim and they're not the very broad-nosed type. They've got quite a lot of Malay blood in them through centuries and centuries of Malays coming across our coast, and some of them looked like wild animal-looking things.

Somewhere or other there's a photo of her there, what betrayed me were her ears. Though I'd made sounds and took a lot of photos of her before... but she heard that click, some very real air current took it to her and she looked round and she was instantly a statue; with arms up like this, doing her hair and showing off what she had to show. She was quite attractive too in a wild way, and she stared and stared and stared, she was paralysed.

I could help grinning after, I had to reassure her and made some silly talk: "It's alright toots, it's alright, I'm not the devil." They're very super-stitious you know, and there's all spirit people about them night and day. She thought I was a spirit devil, God knows what she thought I was going to do to her. She didn't give me a chance to do anything with her. All of a sudden she screamed, she must have jumped six foot, and she almost jumped across that great big water-hole, splashing to the other side. By Christ she was gone in a flash.

Well you see, they've had millions of years to be proud of only them-selves, and how they existed is a mystery of course, against the big animals that were in this country then you see, let alone all sorts of snakes and this sort of bloody thing, and poisonous insects. They were very proud and the only men they had any contact was in the north, the Malay praus that had come along following the *Beche de Mer* - the sea slug. The Chinese mandarins which the ladies in those days used say, were very fond of *Beche de Mer* soup and their praus used to come for the *Beche de Mer*. There were beds of them right up against our coast you see… and the Malays used to land and bargain with the natives - fraternise with them in a way; that's with those tribes that would fraternise. Others only wanted to spear them, and I'm afraid to say some tribes used to put them on the coals too, cut them up.

The best known cannibals were in the big gulf where the Palmer River would go - they used to love the Chinese that swarmed out there. There was 20,000 Chinese round the Cooktown district at one period when the first whites come and they took census. But they used to spit at white men's face because we was too salty, but Chinese was just right. So the poor old chinks used to cop (it), they used to have ten men to guard them – would come out from China when the ships would land in Cooktown the coolies used to pick up their bags and things and away they'd go barefoot; and a couple of armed men would be in the lead with and old-fashioned gun in those days. Great big savage looking Chinese-trained professional soldiers of those days, and a couple at the back, to guard the poor chows from becoming "long pig" - as they were called. It was the name they called them when they roasted Chinamen, that was "long pig". Away they'd go with the armed men guarding them from China because their fare was paid out by groups of Chinese business men and they had one percent of the gold they brought back to China when they made their fortune.

They (Aboriginals) reckoned it was sweeter and more tender. We spoiled our flesh by too much salt, it made them very thirsty the old Aboriginals in those days. They were cruel buggers you know, naturally all stone-age men are in their way, but there was a sort of deficiency in their life. For instance, there was a party of white men…a mob of white prospectors; they ambushed them there was only four or five of them - so they roasted them, clobbered a couple of them and three they slung down and grabbed alive. Well they weren't going to eat the lot, the ones they killed on the day, knocked them on the head and put them in the fire; they ate them... but to keep the others alive they just tore off their clothes and then with a nulla-nulla just cracked their shins. Broke their legs you see, and with the stream there and the palms and the cold water up in among the hills, they just put them in the water, stretched them out there among the stones where the water just flown over them, with their heads above water you see. The cold water kept them cool like we have a machine to put meat in, they kept them there, they were alive. It was live meat for when they wanted them you see, and so they had to lay there while they were dancing and eating the others. Days went by and then they pulled out one bloke and knocked him on the nut with a nulla-nulla, break him up and gradually eat him; the other bloke was waiting for his turn.

One of them, in his swag was a pannikin and a nail and he wrote what they were doing - scratched it you see, and hid the pannikin under a stone thinking blokes would come along and start tracking and that sort of thing. They might find the pannikin which the blokes did when they come looking for them, they didn't know; they just come along and saw where they'd been, found this pannikin where he'd scratched the details: "They've taken Tom now", and it's just a few lines but you could still read it. Those blokes went down their bellies - "long pig".

I was always wary, had to be you see, but not antagonistic. Some of those tribes they'd all be frightened of us and they were terrified of the "thunder gun", and the earliest ones they believed were spirit men, like the Torres Strait Islanders - white men. When they first saw white men... the Aboriginals - the wild ones - were the last stone-age men in the world, other stone-age men had long since seen white men, you see you was what we called sophisticated. But the first white men that the Aboriginals saw - they were spirit men, and they brought down thunder from the heavens from the big storms in the heavens in their shotguns, you see, they were most frightened and terrified of the thunder you see, just like the storms, the thunder was the voice of big spirit men up above to the aboriginals naturally so, and a thunderstorm up there - anywhere, can be terrifying if you don't know any better because someone must make that thunder. Well, it's the thunder God?

In the Kimberleys, they've got the same belief... those are spirit men down from the skies, you see.

11

Lasseter and his Diary

(The Diary) was a pretty cunning thing of Lasseter. Now you can hide nothing from the Aboriginal you see, he's in his native country, and his standing with his bare feet on his own ground, and his eyes that was looking for anything... I mentioned yesterday, his kiddies taught me how to track an ant. Well, Lasseter, he knew he was going to die, he wanted his diary of the day to be saved from the elements, so they could get to his company and to his wife...

He used to put them in a tin and hide them under the ashes in his camp-fire. He'd protect them from the fire and the heat first, as he was building his fire - you see, build deep enough so that he could put a bit of tin down and bark and that to prevent the heat going too far down. He put his fire on and sit there and the natives could watch him having his tucker. There was his fire and when they'd come after him in the morning, they never dreamt that anything was under the camp-fire ashes - that was bloody clever - you know. And night after night, day after day, when he'd have enough of his diaries to hide... naturally they'd never think of anything where there'd been a fire... two bloody fires, they'd never dream anything was under those ashes, my oath!

The Lasseter book? It was only a fluke book too. It was from the police at Alice Springs - it was only a tiny little village in those days. No-one knew of the Alice in those days, they just had a police patrol's camp there. They sent down to Sydney, said they found the body of a prospector. The Aboriginals had told them about a body of a prospector out by this little cave... and I'd read it all in the newspapers. I was down here from the

Harold Lasseter in front of the Central Australian Gold Expedition trucks; Lasseter's Diary as found by Bob Buck in 1931. Idriess purchased this diary from Lasseter's wife and utilised it within Lasseter's Last Ride (1931).

bush with the usual shammy of gold, poor old bugger. I started writing the book seeing that, I thought, "There's a story in that."

This prospector bloke came to this newspaper company and suggested that he found gold out in the Centre. They thought: "Here's a good idea, we'll back him up and he can look for his gold field and still find the route for this road." He was a politician...was it the two Bailey brothers who run "The World" - anyway, it was those three blokes who backed him, but that was the whole idea, that's how he got money.....

I found this out, going wandering about and making enquiries, I went down to the Mines Department, I think (it was) they who put me right, they said: "Oh yes, that prospector, the proprietors of *The World's News*, it was the daily of those days. So I went and saw them and they told me all about it and got me to the police chaps and right up some of them, because I wanted to send him (George Warnecke) some more you see. That's where I got the whole idea from.

Then when the police sent them down the diary, my publishers they looked at me, as something they couldn't understand... I had only written three or four books but they'd each been best-sellers, and this bloody Wild Man from Borneo - from the bush. Of course they didn't believe in me at all, they reckoned it's not possible, the story can't be that (real), and the Australian people actually bought Australian books - Australian booksellers actually bought after the first bloody book...unheard of.

I found out from them (at the *World*), they told me all that they knew and how they'd financed him. When the police eventually sent us down any papers and that sort of thing, that was when they got the news of the old bushie up there, dug under the ashes of Lasseter's fire spot, there was his bloody diaries under the fire spot. Old Buck[19] - He lived on for years ever since on his reputation...

But Lasseter left the diaries behind in every camp-fire did he?
Yes.
Not just dug them up and took them away again?
Oh no, no.
And who was the old boy that discovered the diaries?
Bob Buck, Buck you see. And he used to put on a tree "HB" - just chop a bit with a tomahawk, that was another good guide.

Do you believe that the reef exists?

I think it did. But my idea was much more north to where they've been looking for it. Because north I know well, I've been up there… the further north up along the overland telegraph line looking west, the more minerals you can see - the granite country, slate country. To a prospector that means a chance of minerals you see, whereas the way they've gone looking for it according to the photos on television, it doesn't look like mineral country at all to me.

It was through that the last big goldfield in Australia was found - Tennant Creek. The old boy (Kenneth Stuart [20]) had previously bought this prospecting book by some bloody unknown Aussie bloke but he reckons it was pretty good, and when he heard of Lasseter's reef he thought to himself: "Christ, I know that old bugger so well, I've been in his station there again and again." He got the idea: "Well I don't know if there's any truth in this bloody *Lasseter's Last Ride* or not but this gold is good." He started sending the natives out - I nearly said a terrible word then - to pick up the heaviest rocks they could find, break off little bits of them and bring them to him, and he'd give them half a stick Nicky-Twist tobacco - that's trade tobacco - it means fuck?? …and in Africa it's called "trade tobacco"- that's sweepings of the tobacco floors, you get chips and spit and Christ knows what-not…

Us diggers when we go out in the bush and run out of tobacco we used to break the awful looking stuff up and bloody well smoke it: "Any port in a storm" as the monkey said when…anyway what the hell was I talking about?

Anyway these boys found the pinnacles of a reef… and then he'd dolly up these stones from the *Prospecting for Gold* book and wash them (in) Tennant Creek - It was blessed, in the old worn-out creek of ancient days it had a great big water-hole and it was never known to go dry. When the Overland Telegraph line was built the main station was built there, where there'd always been water in this waterless country…

So he'd wash down there, and one day he got a trace of yellow gold… he found specks and lumps in a water dish and all. Of course it was a great pastime for a lonely man like that, see. He knew an old prospector 300 miles to the south… and told him just what he'd found and said:

"I'll grub-steak you out of my salary if you'd like to come and have a look round." So the old fossicker did and the natives took him out these heavy bloody stones, had a hell of a job finding his right place again… he was virtually legless, then he dug a trench through a crest of a hill and there was the gold right enough - that was Tennant Creek, the start of Tennant Creek.

Lasseter was much more likely to have found that you see, right in his line of travel, but to the north in gold country. I think that it very likely that that was what he found; then wandering when he went sick and lost his sight while the natives would still have him. God knows where he wandered to. They found him by this little cove because he had to follow (wherever) the natives would lead him. He couldn't direct them to go any-where, he just had to go where they went hunting for their tucker. That's what I think had happened. He went with them until they left him to die - that's what they do with their own people, they generally leave them a drop of water and a kangaroo bone. It's nature… they couldn't have weak and sick people on their hands in those arid sort of country, especially if it's in a drought time.

These men of Charoo, spirit and sun worshippers, shook with terror at the sight of horses and mules. An Idriess photograph from *Our Living Stone Age,* 1963.

1 2

On Travelling with Aboriginals

I wouldn't take pictures in any wild place I've been, not until they got used to me and trusted me - you see. If I had horses or if I was travelling with a patrol and we'd usually have a long string of mules, I'd have a few tomahawks with me but particularly pipes and what they'd love above anything, a few cases of this Nicky Twist trade tobacco. The big people who supplied the tobacco here and Melbourne and Western Australia, made handy little cases about that deep from that deep - usen't to cost us much, but it had quite a lot of "knicki-knicki" tobacco in it in sticks...

Christ! you know, I've got some sticks here. Do you know, out of curiosity - to see how long it'd really last. When I was 42 years of age I brought some down to Sydney with me, and I used to save up all my old pipes, they was valuable when you're right out in the bush because the natives would love the pipe. I used to smoke a pipe and then I'd put them aside for when I was in wild native country again - I brought some of these down to Sydney with me and when I finally stayed down here and used to only go out every years for six months, twelve months...two years as the case might be, I'd take those things with me, but I still had some left when I settled down altogether here. I come across them the other day, they're in one of my drawers in there...

Oh yes, I always got on well with the Aboriginals (in the Kimberleys), I seemed to get on quietly (with them), I never used to laugh at them. A lot of the blokes used to ask them point-blank about their spirit beliefs and that sort of thing, and then they'd think it was very smart - the white blokes - he'd laugh, shout out to the others: "Oh, him believe in some spirit man jump up, when he die Jacky jump up all them as white man";

which were their beliefs when I was a boy...They're strong in reincarnation, their spirits are less than strong in reincarnation, but they're all sensible bloody beliefs, more sensible than these blokes who laughed at them, who didn't have any bloody beliefs. But you mustn't laugh at them, they're nearly as badly hurt as the whites, and if you laugh at a white man, you hurts his bloody great ego don't you?

Oh no, I'd never laugh at them. And when they'd show me anything - any wildlife of interest or any interesting looking stone, I'd take much interest even if I'd seen them before, and knew more about it perhaps than they did themselves. I got on with them very well indeed from the start.

Now that put me in the position as I got to know them more and more and travelled more and more, you gradually began to see what their beliefs were and to understand them, and you got out of that terrible fix which a lot of blokes, the professional anthropologists even used to fall to it naturally, The Aboriginal is quite smart in his own way and he always wants to please the white man if there's a tomahawk or a pound of tobacco in it or anything to eat, or let alone a dress for his gin. He finds out from his cobbers, they all tell one another what the white man likes, what he wants. As the bloody population spread, they've got to know more and more of what the white man would like them to say they believe. A lot of this stuff that they thought had been printed in books you see. You can easily understand it because the white man would be delighted, one of his fond beliefs of what these barbarian savages believe is already felt by most of you.

As they got more sophisticated you see... like new strange young blokes going out studying anthropology for the first time, a hell of a lot of them got caught. I'd learnt that even as a boy, even round about Lismore I learnt a lot of those tricks from the cunning old Aboriginals there - my cobbers down at the creek, and their know-all old mothers...by Christ! They were real Tarzans those old gins down there.

They've let me see some of their different rights and that sort of thing, after over half of a lifetime, of travelling and among them, often I'd go out with them in places where it'd be a difficulty to get a horse and that sort of thing...and I'd bring along tucker: "You take me up to so and so," up the mountain. I've travelled with them and slept in little gunyahs. I can make a gunyah myself nearly as good as the gin - not as good, but quite good enough for a sudden storm; and I've slept in with them and their mangy dogs who come calling in to sleep too. A little bit of gunyah packed with men - hubby and his wives and that, and there'd be another one near you and all their piccaninnies.

And that bloody smoke, they wouldn't cut a hole in to let it bloody well escape up there, they'd breathe down close to the ground. Any draft would keep the air clean but the humidity and sweat and heat and especially if it was pouring rain in the wet season outside, the steam off these bloody awful dogs - poor mangy wretches. By God it was pretty tough on nights like that. If it wasn't raining outside, I'd just camp outside on my blanket, but I've slept under those conditions for weeks on some trips. And at other times we might be caught going in on their tribal land and that and there's a couple of gunyahs handy and the Aboriginals would know we'd get in, in case of a sudden shower... So I got to know them very well right from babyhood down.

The travelling was what did it because every tribe has got something different within it, and some are intelligent and some pity the white man that was intelligent; but they had the intelligence alright. Do you know that I mentioned that witch doctor who discovered penicillin, it was not (discovered by) white people at all, he'd known it for a hundred years.

Penicillin, we reckon we only found it out yesterday don't we? The Aboriginals used penicillin for unknown thousands of years probably - certainly hundreds. I'd been travelling along with a mob of natives... they've got to keep on the go because of hunting - you see, animals will only live for certain time with the hunters, they go for new hunting grounds. When the Aboriginal picks up his spear and woomera, he'll go hunting in their tracks you see sort of thing... well me, I used to be always hunting with cobbers for gold and that sort of thing, well we'd often travel with natives who'd kid us about "Oh, big heavy stone so and so." We'd travel with them to have a look, to make sure - because goldfields had been found like that, particularly the black tin field, that used to attract their eyes for some reason, more than gold. I've often wondered if it was the colour - stream tin is jet-black and their colour is jet-black...God knows.

With the natives is always one or two in the family way and they travel along - her time comes, well then they wait for a little while, the mob would go further along, they might get some wild honey… and don't wait too long for the poor devil. Of course if it's in dry time they'd go straight on, you must keep up or else, see, that's life out in the drastic country, in short rainfall and drought time. Well, always their women friends would stop with the women (in child-birth) while the other women went on carrying their stuff. I used to want to see what was doing, all ways in their life I was interested…Well, the women would scoop a hole, say two feet deep, do it out easy, come to a patch of sand somewhere, easy scoop it out. Other woman would light a fire and heat rocks, especially flat rocks and the sort of rocks that would absorb heat…they'd get kindling, fill with bushes, light a strong fire and put the rocks on and get them practically red hot. When the woman's time (to give birth) came she'd kneel over with a part of here all opened to that heat. They'd get that green scum that occurs on a lot of pools of water, that scum that floats about. There were different sorts of green leaves. They'd pick it just with their hands and put it in the bark of the Coolamon. Part of this green scum had different properties and when these stones would go red hot, they'd throw in handful over handfuls on to these red-hot stones. Up would come steam straight away, that was steam of penicillin, and the woman would just have her baby and she'd kneel over it and fanned this steam up into herself where she was all bleeding - that'd stop blood poisoning. That's why they didn't all die over blood poisoning, that was penicillin, steam of penicillin - my oath!

There's lots of things like that about the Aboriginals…all sort of beliefs and some of them are quite right too. They didn't think vast things out like the whites or other natives that had great populations all mixing together in one tribe and telling one another because they had to keep to small tribal numbers - because of the small game resources compared to Africa and those places.

Australia was floating along on its own and the rest of the world knew nothing about it, so they had no knowledge whatsoever except what nature pushed in front of them and they had to find out how to survive. That's why they didn't have a great repertoire but believe me they have got a repertoire where bad language is concerned. If you heard those natives swearing at one another, the most atrocious cuss words when they get mad - you know, the gins go for one another with the fighting sticks for cracking the skull - poor devils, till one drops down with concussion. You hear them scream and the men throw the language at one another before they start at one another with their waddys - they're shocking. They shocked me! After a row, I got some of the natives to tell me what did so and so call Jacky so and so - when they'd tell me it'd raise my head and scalp: "Oh, you dirty, stinkin', fuckin', bloody, rotten bastard. Kiss me arse you bastards!"

Well, it was shocking. And some expressions I couldn't make out what they meant, God knows what part of the anatomy. The gins, worse than the men. They'd fight. Oh they were terrors when they did fight. All that saved them from dying out in the gin's fights was to make themselves beautiful, with this long, straggly hair they had, they'd sit down if they was near a pool with nice clay, nice mallee clay that you can make things out of, and put great daubs of clay in their hair, cat-tails to their hair, so their head was covered with an armoury. When it got hard well there was armour in front and back... and the waddys would come down on this clay ....Crack! You could hear it ringing with the hard clay and the waddys, and they couldn't get to their skulls until they'd broken a lot of these clay things, by Christ!

Every gin in any tribe, it was as common among them...that's part of their custom. When they decided to fight, the tribe would look on, they've got to stand out there in the middle and every gin has a gin's digging stick, it's a waddy about that long...with a fire-hydrant end and a fire-hydrant knob at the other end to crack things...crack hard nuts and shellfish and this sort of thing. That's their fighting stick. So each one has got take a bang for a bang, they've got to bend down like this and the other stands in front and up with this awful thing and down! Fair on her head. Then she'd stagger over, pick herself up, gets her breath and then the other has got to bend down and by Christ, don't she get herself balanced to swing all the way, to get her own back and more of the one she's fighting there.

A lot of them crack themselves inside and die in misery perhaps in years to come. Brain damage... poor things. But what used to save them from the fight were these big hard clay balls, the sun-hardened them like rock, the hair all dangling with these huge clay balls - when they shake their bloomin' heads you could hear them rattling like stones rattling together...

Japanese diver in weighted boots about to go down
off Broome, 1910.
Captain Ancel Gregory, Broome.

1 3

Forty Fathoms Deep

I was great friends with a Captain Gregory [21] one of the better-known captains of all the pearling fleets. He was known even on Thursday Island, which was the other great pearling centre. The skipper was in Broome which was then romanticlly but rightfully called, "The City of Pearls". It was a wonderful place the Broome of those days. The white people with the nice bungalows and the Japanese there had a big society - it was the Japanese that used to take many of the pearling boats out. The Japanese skippers had a society place and a well organised society, and their seamen where Koepangers from one of the Malay principalities. The Koepangers and the Chinese had a business part of the town and were very knowledgeable. Quiet but very shrewd businessmen the Chinese merchants were, believe me.

It was lovely city there away from the bare desert country on the coast. We even had a Bishop's ghost there. We had a Bishop who governed in his spiritual way an area of country nearly as big as Europe, he used to control all the north and the coastline. He had his palace there, it was a very nice bungalow, but it was called the Bishop's Palace. The bishop had a ghost - and me and the old hoodoo man spent night after night when the bishop was away in the interior... we used to be sleeping on his verandah waiting for this damned ghost...

Captain Gregory was an old English navy man, and he left the navy many years. He'd been in so many cyclones he was well known for managing a schooner... it don't matter now because I'm afraid he's passed out to the seas up above, if there's any on those comets up above, but he was also working all the time with the Australian Secret Service.

Our defence was well looked after in those days. One of the pearling captains got me to do a tiny little job for the same Secret Service when this war was coming on. But anyway, he was a real Secret Serviceman, and well is his work in sailing this big ship (the *Redbill*). He was a man of many adventures, he was known all over the pearling world of those days, which was a very rigourous world.

When the pearl beds were first found which was way down more towards...I think it was down towards Shark Bay, down towards Broome, the pearls and the shells used to be often in shallow water in those days like the shells that took their places. I used to wade out and get these North West luggers... the shells took their places in the shallow water and then when the deep beds were found; there was a diving dress. It was a very clumsy thing, vastly different to the diving suit we have today, the chaps would have loved to have had this dress that you see on television now.

You had to go down in very thick heavy rubber watertight suit with boots. Each of the boots were 20 pounds weight, I know they felt like a ton when you put them on, you could barely move on a schooner to get down (into the water). The crew had to help me over the side. I used to go down more for curiosity, I was no bloody good in looking for pearl-shell wandering about down there, and the crocodiles would be up here chasing mice. When you go down... you've got to find great big pearl-shells in reefs down below covered with all sorts of weird plants and plant-animals all gently waving in the tide... When you're a newcomer like me there are some nasty things there. There's one sea-snake that hides in there, if you put your hand on him you're a going to die in a matter of minutes. There's hundreds of sorts of sea-snakes...they go like hell from you but this one can kill you and the stonefish too, he's a terrible agony that damned thing; he don't move, he just puts his spikes out....

The native divers from the islands used to manage these suits quite easily, but they'd have to walk about in them... and make sure that your breathing line didn't get entangled with the tide under strips of coral. It's like precipices down below, only all sorts of shapes, not clean-cut. There's all sorts of shapes up above you and round about you and your two life-lines connected up above, you can hear the "thump, thump" of the blokes with the pump, pumping air down there, and that long air- line you can see its shadow going right up and you can see the bottom of the lugger on top of the bright sky. You can clearly see the bottom of the lugger and the only thing connecting you to that is this lifeline - your airline and if that gets entangles up...Oh, you lose it, you're a gonner.

They had many accidents with the paralysis. The bends. They'd go down too deep - you see, the deeper you went the less other divers had been there... like prospectors had to go up in the wild country to get a chance of gold or tin, well the deeper they went they better the chance they'd get for pearls. They'd go just too deep and get a terrible thing, that paralysis thing. I've seen them on Thursday Island as well as Broome. And in later years someone invented a thing (decompression chamber) you could send down to them and they could lower or make higher the pressure from the lugger's deck. You'd come up foot by foot, you'd have to wait half an hour and then another half an hour and another half hour to get the oxygen back in your lungs.

Every day was a delight looking for gold inland, no matter if you're sweating all day long and you didn't get a speck of gold in an hour or for the next two or three months, you were alive and anytime you might strike again. You always were sure you were going to bloody well strike it. He always lived in hope - the prospector, even if he died in despair - which most of them did. But now and again, my mates and me, we'd strike a few tons of tin or a few ounces of gold or a few opals, depending what we was looking for and where we were in the continent. Then it was alive.

FORTY
FATHOMS DEEP.
PEARL DIVERS & SEA ROVERS
IN AUSTRALIAN SEAS.

By Ion L. Idriess.

Abbott Street, Cairns in 1919, when the Spanish Flu hit
the North Queensland Peninsular.
Japanese postcard 1910.

14

The Wildest parts of the Bush

In my day I'd just pick up my gun and my horse and away I'd go and something was bound to happen in no time you see. I'd go to the wildest part of the bush to go sandalwood cutting up the west-coast. The natives were really bad down there but we treated them, made arrangements with them first...I'd be coming with the whole team's load of tucker, you arrived and then you made friends with all those natives in the part of the coast you were going. They'd see you weren't interrupted by any other mob - not until they go what you had and you didn't let them have the last of that until you got your sandalwood and was out of there...

What spoilt the peninsular was that terrible thing the Spanish Flu. That's where we got it, in that lonely place, long before you got it down here, the Spanish Flu it came straight down the peninsular. It gave one a terrible thirst and heat. I've seen the sweat running off as if it was water running off the duck's back, and the first thing an Aboriginal does or any white person when he's hot is run into cold water. That's the very worst thing, I've seen them in some hundreds up in the beaches up in the peninsular, washing in and out with the tide where they'd run down to lie in the water. They'd die in there with whatever the disease turned into with this water… pneumonia I suppose. All down that coast-line it must have wiped out more than half of the thick native population, because there was tucker everywhere there, they had no need of birth control.

My oath they were pretty bloody rough I can assure you, but it had to be, believe me. You could like, embrace your wife and that's okay, but you wouldn't have any chance of a baby. Yes, the "whistle cock" (the sub-incision of the penis). By God! They let me watch that a few times... and if you made the least squeal - you weren't a man; then the boy had to go back and be with women, go walkabout with the women, be a carrier for them, he wasn't a man...Gees, what a man would do for his missus...

I had too much interest in the mineral type of life (than to take up a selection). I liked travelling. I liked wandering the coast too and that takes up time... When I was a boy, working for five bob a week from before dawn till after sundown, milking those bloody cows. I could have had an opal field but I left them there and... got hooked up with women see. I thought I've found the most marvellous specimen of a girl in the world while I was travelling... I got the flamin' opals around me neck and I still went back to the bush... I'd go to Western Australia, the Kimberleys and then move about, get horses from the stations along the only road they had to come back into.... meet some trapper...

There was always a trapper going backwards and forwards, especially in the cattle business. I'd be in the city six months and then twelve months or so out in the bush again, collecting stories and copy for Christmas time... If I have to write books for a living I better do it the right way and I'm sure the people like what I found out, they like true stuff you see. All of my stuff was of just wandering about like that, it's so simple, but the people liked it too right so they had their (own) little bit of adventure.

15

Pearl Diving off Thursday Island

I first went down in the Thursday Island waters. The diving suit is very heavy and very heavy boots to keep you down against the tide. You go down very slowly, you land on your tootsies but you've got to have heavy boots and a heavy suit because the current is strong down there. You'd never dream it from up top but according to the weather and the seasons of the year the current can be very strong and it can wash you in among the coral which is very dangerous. You've got your air pipeline going up and it's like cliffs all around you - jagged cliffs. Sometimes you see all the devil's own head but a great big fat devil he is with eyes as big as saucers - green, glaring at you from the coral - that's the giant Groper and his got a mouth... like a bloomin' great big balloon split in half...full of jagged teeth. He's a terrible looking brute when he gapes at you with his great jaws opening now and again… you see their jaws gaping, the flash of their teeth. A lot of them they're just inhaling this plankton, there's billions of tiny things floating about - clouds of them sometimes, in the water and they're food for a lot of fishes. The (Groper's) gills - they're a sort of sponge. They absorb the foodstuff and close down on it and squirt out the carcases…

A lot of them are very curious and they're not frightened of man down below… they're a damned nuisance because they'd be butting in at your helmet, trying to get at your face. I suppose they think it's something... have a bite out of this...and this cheeky looking snout is "butt, butt, butt" against the blasted helmet, and a lot of them travel in clouds, and you've got packs of them swimming beside you : "Get the hell out of it you stupid goats", push them out of your road and then they swim straight in again.

I used to get as wild as anything because I'd be particularly interested in prying for pearl-shell among the coral … but you've got the find the pearl-shell and you wouldn't think you'd be using your eyes so much down below when you're all under water but by cripes you do. That's where you see things down below, but you've got to get light to see these.

The further you go down the duller it gets of course but you don't go down that far otherwise you'd get the bends. There is light and it filters and when you see the pearl-shell up in the reef, there's just a mass of plants and animals, weedy things all waving out at you. It's like trying to find some tiny thing in a huge garden, only this is much worse because it's sort of dark moonlight sort of world down there, and all these things reaching out at…I don't know what they are, but you catch a glint down (there)… while you're looking for pearl-shell what's that glint you see? Now pearl-shells come with all sorts of crawling, creepy things and grass growing on it and all, so (the glint) you see - it's a pearl-shell having its daily tucker. It's got its sort of lips where its shell closes, stubby sort of lips… and the tiny little bit of opening is pearl-shell. The lips are pearl-shell in the shell, and they glint just like what they are - pearl, and you see these tiny little glint in there among the dense grey, blue-green reef - it's gone in a flash, and there's another one way out there and another there, you'll know your in a mob of pearl-shells. You've still got to watch out for that little glint and grab with your hands and make bloody sure you don't grab any nasty thing as much as you can. And then that pearl-shell is covered with lots of plant… on almost all there's grasses of some sort. Well, you've got to get that and it's a great big thing, the big pearl-shell are as big as say, the small plate on the table, those small ceramic plates you put your bread and butter on - they're as big as that and flat, and heavy. About one or two or three pounds weight - you see, it's very heavy pearl-shell, and then pass by a byssus that's all heavy strands where it grows to the coral reef and it clings there, and defies all naughty fishes trying to wrench it away to eat it.

That's the pearls and you've got to rinse them, you've got a sort of basket round your waist, all holes in it where water can go. Fill this (basket) up and then signal the diver with the line and he sends down the rope and the hook and up she goes and you never see them again, and so you carry on… You've got to learn what is that momentary glint of pearl because

Thursday Island luggers.
Thursday Island settlement, both early 1920s.

you'll come to another reef and you'll see numerous wonder these little glints but they're different, they don't close in a second. After a while you see them coming out and poking themselves at you, and you wonder what the hell this is till you wake up of course - it's a great big sea-crayfish and that's his eye, these little sparkly pearls...coming out at you to have a look at this gawky-looking thing.

They used to lose, comparatively speaking, quite a number of diver. Any man learning a new trade or a new type of work, he gets to know what he can do and what he mustn't do. It's the same way down below, and with the native divers of course, they'd know straight away. It was the white men that used to suffer most because it took them time to learn - the white divers - just how deep they could go without being in danger. The Torres Strait Islanders for instance, were the best divers and the Malays that they imported, they'd been in the water from babyhood. Their mothers and fathers teach them how far they could go down, but with the white man coming up there and learning in those days well, everything was danger to him, and they wouldn't understand the bottom. It'd be like a man going out in the bush for the first time, he'd have to know how to find this way through the bush - it's the same down below, you could step on what looked like the sea bottom but it'd be a big hole covered with growing sort of things and you'd go down and out of your depth - and you could easily then get your lifelines caught. You had to learn those things.

Some divers made real good divers among the whites but as the years went by they found that there was less accidents - much less - with the Torres Strait Islanders and with the coastal Japanese, they're used to water... the Japanese divers, the Malays and the Torres Strait Islanders - they knew their way about through boyhood, whereas any white races weren't used to that. They had to have fatalities before they learnt how to look at what are the danger zones. And there's lots of coral growths you could put your hands with immunity in, among them others would be dangerous... Stonefishes are likely to be in the reef, you'd put your hand on one of them...Oh, it'd be awful.

It's just like everything else in life, it's a new world altogether and you've got to learn your way about it if you go down there, especially up in the Barrier Reef... It's just a paradise of life, all sorts of fishes and snakes and eels and things like that... eels everywhere, you can see their heads gleaming - that's (when) all their teeth opened, when they're sucking in stuff, and waiting for a fish to pass their home. They dive out with those awful damned teeth... you only meet sheer accidents like that if you slip and you put your hand out and it happens to be near his hole, he thinks you're after him - he'll grab you just like a nanny goat. You could walk right over a snake and all he'll want to do is get away from you but if you kick at him or hit at him he snaps... same down below. Some fish will go at you, some of the big barracuda tribes... and they've got terrible teeth they'll make a snap and have a bit out of you. Of course, once there's blood the sharks come along... there's a hell of a lot more accidents here in these civilized streets with cars not looking where you're going and that sort of thing than there are down there...roaming the sea bottom there's not nearly so many as there roaming the city streets.

Cane cutters at Ayr, North Queensland,1907 postcard.
Cane-cutters at the Kamai Estate near Ayr in 1910.

16

The Hardest Job in the Bush

The hardest jobs I've ever found in the bush or in all my wandering life - it flamin' was cane-cutting among your own cobbers. They're the biggest task-masters I've ever met - the buggers, because you form your own gangs - you used to in my day - and you elect your own boss, the boss that's responsible to the mill of the cane or to the farmer who has the field. But you contract to do your very best by your mates and your boss, and that boss - he's elected by everyone to be the best cane-cutter that they know - the swiftest. Of course the more you cut - it's contract work like shearers - and you've got to keep up with the boss or your own cobbers sack you that night: "I'm sorry Jack...", like they said to me the bastards! I nearly broke my back keeping up with those blokes for two or three weeks and I'd had it, you know, I said: "Thank Christ! I will be saying to 'Hell with you', I wouldn't say thanks, you and your bloody mob!"

You're out there, you're standing with your cane knife and it's cold as bloody ice and your waiting for the first glimmer of dawn to come and here's the ganger in your middle and you're a line of poor shivering wretches to each side of him. By the first streak of dawn his left hand reaches out and grabs a dirty stinking slimy ice-coned big stick of cane in one hand, bend it across himself and down with his knife and your knife has got to hit the butt of that cane exactly the same time as him. Then the next step another stick of cane down...from before bloomin' proper dawn light till it's too dark or you'd cut your toes off.

The hardest job in the bush. Then you've got you pick up when you're done, you've got to cart those canes on your shoulder, pick up as many as you can till the last cane and stagger down to the river bank to the punt or wherever you're putting them all in a mob to market. When you load the punts up, dirty great punt out there with a long plank on it - and as a team, one after the other you've got these heavy weights! You're like a camel and you've got to go down this plank, and it's bouncing - you know, bouncing like blazes and if you slip off, oh blimey!

Better to go gold prospecting - yes, and you're on this dear old thing we call "land" - my oath! When you're on that bouncy sea you don't know from one hour to another what is going to happen, it might be absolutely beautiful and romantic...beautiful blue sea and islands and island girls within reach of the boat and that sort of thing. You might have a fishing line while the other boys is down looking for the bloomin' old pearling reef and in another hour that boat is up and down, up and down. You've got to go out to sea or else that lovely island that you can see - you'll be washed up against the reef there... On land anywhere, when the storms come you've got your tent or a rock or some shelter or you can build a gunyah like the Aboriginals do, quick and lively - when you learn how to you know. There's shelter always somewhere, anyway you're not washed out to sea to be food for the sharks if you hit a coral reef...no, give me the land every time.

I don't like repeating things and I like the bush, but I don't like going back on my tracks. I'd never go back on my tracks now of course. What was real wild interesting places in my day there's now towns or houses, or a road built. There was no roads for the prospectors - you see, because you wanted to keep away from any land that had been opened up or developed. The wilder the country the more untamed it was, the more chance of gold or tin or wolfram or minerals.

We used to keep to the wild way and to me that was always the more interesting, the wild Aboriginals was always of interest... right back to the stone-age man, which is much more interesting than a half civilized man or a civilized man. It was to me anyway and my cobbers.

Of course the very stuff we were looking for - the mineral was new. When you pick up a bit of gold it wasn't just from a new creek you got the first gold that was ever taken out by a man, which was different to buying something...When you see it, it is, when you pick it up absolutely new and yours and yodel: "Stone the crows! Eureka!" By cripes life was interesting.

Right up in the north, we come across some quickly flowing little river going hell for leather as a lot of the coastal rivers do after the rainy season. You'd see great a big fat old crocodile there, and say: "Well I saw you first, I'm not going near you, but I'm the first white man you ever seen, and if I can get my rifle out of the pack-saddle you'd know all about it." By that time he says: "What's this damned thing, I can't get it and I don't like the look of it", and he slides straight down the mud and he's flopped into the creek and away.

I used to test those things, I've seen them take young gins...One day in the Daintree a young gin with a baby on her back come in to use the river, which had a big wooden affair to get water with a pail - and as soon as she looked down, still a little close enough to be around that water-hole, up comes this great croc. Grabbed both her and her baby and do you know, he flopped straight back into the water. She got away, she got away. I was standing on the other side of the damned river and I couldn't fire because the woman and the baby were in his mouth, and the huge big body is swishing all around. It was no good standing, just aiming at it, I had to be sure. She jabbed her thumbs in his eyes and kept gouging and screwing... if you imagine that in your own eyes it's the most terrible pain... the same with the bloody crocodile only, she was gouging deep into him. It was her only chance and he had her body, part of the baby and part of her in his bloomin' jaws.... He let go, and she managed to struggle ashore and scream and the warriors come running down with their spears. Too bloody late of course, but she got out of it.

And the baby survived, some of the teeth had just gone through it's little ribs and crushed them, but both mother and baby got over it...yeah.

The Broken Hill Proprietary Company mine where Idriess worked as a boy.
A Western Australian Aboriginal showing initiation scarring, 1923.

17

Just an Australian Barbarian

Over the last six or eight years I saw the entire coast was encircled with mining ventures – (in areas) well, what used to be wild, and it's taken a lot of my interest, for chaps like me or timber getters for new timber country or for new land to take up for a cattle station. All us blokes - well, those opportunities are now gone practically - you see, so you've got to think of other ways.

Well I was very fond of chemistry before I left Broken Hill. I was in the Broken Hill Proprietary Essay Office, and we then had to go to the School of Mines at the technical college and night school learning metallurgy and essaying and I got fascinated then - not only to look for minerals like I spent most of my life but for the things minerals can do and what minerals there are in rocks. There's any amount of discoveries to be made in metallurgy and the chemical part of mining and processing - and that occupies a man if he can take an interest in it, can occupy his life because man… especially if he's making a living out of practical purposes the more interested and contented he is… Say a sportsman of the top class that make thousands, tennis playing their life or footballing or whatever it is and they want to be a top man. His life is occupied so he's got something. If a man hasn't got anything much in his mind, well what the bloody hell is the good of being alive anyway if there's nothing in his life.

Now thinking about going into the bottom of the sea and walking about there and exploring the bottom of the sea - which a man can do with all these modern things, he's going to be able to walk along the sea bottom with his own oxygen, without cumbersome diving dresses and with safety.

I'm on the way out now but I wonder that I don't see in our harbour some simple invention to put on your feet and walk across the bloody harbour... that'll come sometime, some simple thing on your feet containing say, condensed air or air under pressure to holdup your weight. Something to stop our boats in the North from going head over heels. A new keel... a bit of keel on it for the balance and the weight sorted. I wonder why some simple thing like that hasn't been discovered years ago.

There's so many discoveries that have been made since my day in metallurgy and the treatment of ores. For years and years Australia's sold to England but particularly Germany who I think...were then the cleverest chemists in the world, now... I think Australian metallurgists have since proved that they are even (more) clever than the Germans by virtue of the great discoveries in the hope...starting from the Broken Hill Proprietary and the Zinc Corporation gold. Oh the British people who had the shares used to say, all Broken Hill ores went to Germany, in ships that weren't ours - good luck to them they were enterprising people.

It took the Aussies quite a time to find out how the Germans did it, they had such clever metallurgical chemists that could extract not only the silver and lead which was what those ores were sold for but they used to get about 20 minerals out of every ton. It'd be 20 more than what they paid for, and the little bit that they didn't even count on paying for it was so little the gold percentage of the ores, it was supposed to be just the silver and the lead. The Germans got out of the gold alone all the costs of those ships and those shipments and all the rest was profit out of this tiny little percentage - well that was the metal...that was finding out what was in those stones and how to get all the good stuff of it. Well now there's so many ores...there's more to be found out and better and easier processes to be found, and the mineral world alone it's terrific for opportunities...

We made a big name for ourselves far more than we know and the wide-awake European countries they know now that we have got brains in everything - in every profession. Somewhere in the world an Australian is right up among the very top.

All over the world there's Australians in engineering, electricity - and these new chemical discoveries. He's a leader in every country in the world, we don't understand that yet but we're going to increasingly take a big part in any new chemical profession or industrial or electronic (processing) in the world. We'll be among the foremost, instead of being thought of as barbarians by the high and mighty Europeans and Britain and all the rest of them.

My old man always called me till the last: "Just an Australian barbarian."

I used to say to him: "Never you mind about being an Australian barbarian...an Aboriginal barbarian savage, it's my great-great grandfather on your side used to knock them out with a club in one hand and paint yourself with woad (ochre) just like our Aboriginals do." And strangely enough, I've learnt that in Britain they reckon we've got a slang of our own. Well, you get a mob of Britishers among you - in the army, we couldn't understand their yabber with a lot of them, and anytime we had a spell, meet them in Cairo where we'd have beers...Some blokes would say: "What the bloody hell are they yabbering about these blokes?" – and they've got the cheek to say that we've got a tag (in our mouths)...

They've got a little island and had six hundred tribes and those tribes among them (were) the Wessexes and the so-and-so Shires and this Shire and that - they're all the relics of tribes. Strangely enough (when) they counted the Aboriginals years and years ago here, they managed to count up just over six hundred tribes of Aboriginals. Yet these pommies have got the cheek to say: "Oh, they've all got an Australian tag." They're damned cheeky.

WOOMERA SPEARSMAN, NORTH QUEENSLAND.

Aboriginal tribesman, Bloomfield area, 1910.

1 8

Men of the Jungle

Only one favourite book - *Men in the Jungle,*[22] for certain reasons... I was gold-mining near the Bloomfield River out at China Camp, that's only about a hundred miles south of Cooktown. If we had horse we'd go overland, over the mountains and there was only one track and oh, it was terrible difficult for the horses. So the easiest way was to go by pearling lugger to Pierce's Landing up the Bloomfield River, and we'd land there and then ride overland from there, borrow horses from Pierce's...Well the Bloomfield is a beautiful river, it's only a short river, it enters towards the coast over some low falls - very pretty as all falls are, but both banks are wild. It's a tropical river, then over what they call the Wyalla Plains, and a wild, wild Plain it was in my days. Only tracks through the grass across that Plain and the grass would be over your head. You had to keep throwing out your arms - you see, and any moment you'd get a stupid mob of wild pigs trying to get a bit of sunlight on the bare track - and they bloody started scampering, squealing with a pig jumping up and at you. By Christ it's an experience and you've got to be careful too near the big river because crocodiles, (they) often go on land and wait in places like that for wallabies hopping along - You see, wallabies make a track like wild pigs make a track and they lie just in the wallabies track, who makes his last hop right into these great open jaws.

The settlements there at the mouth of the Bloomfield River had always interested me, like people in the Islands. There were the Malays and Chinese and Island girls and believe me they're lovely island girls - they were fascinating people to me and they're so friendly, and of course some of them have known me from different islands. When I was looking for pearl-shell and that, it was delightful. We'd sit under the mango trees, a mob of us under the stars when they'd come out and we'd be all in a group singing and dancing, playing the banjo and enjoying life. By cripes you could enjoy your life on that beautiful river there, and if you wanted fish, just pick up a fish-spear. In a matter of moments, Jack would go to the banks of the river and it was teaming with fish, you never thought of such fish. If you wanted a banana reach out your hand and pull one off the banana trees growing everywhere - you had your choice of all sorts of tropical fruit. It was hard to make up your mind which fruit you'd choose. Pineapples - just pick them and chop them with a cane knife and start eating them straight away.

It was an idyllic time and those coloured people of all shades from a golden pink to a golden russet and by cripes they looked good you know - under those surroundings anyway. And the men were very interesting, they knew a bit about minerals because mineral camps weren't very far away and they were great fishermen. They knew all about pearl-shell and other shells too.

90

19

On Cooktown and the Pierce Brothers

Arthur Pierce was a very shrewd serious-minded little chap, he used to look after the lugger and go backwards and forwards from Cooktown with other settlement's goods. Arthur looked after the cattle station, the Pierces had taken up a lot of land from the river right through to China Camp and they used to be great favourites with the local natives and he was training up the stockmen. He was wild and woolly, didn't have a care in the world. You'd say to him: "A bull is among them, see if you can round him up." He was pretty wild too Arthur. Arthur let out a wild "Whoo!" and went straight into the scrub after this bloody bull. He didn't want the damned old bull but just the chase, and bloody well, he'd go into anything. By cripes we used to like him, but he was always into something.

He tried to get me to swim my horse across the big cataract. Backwards is the Roaring Meg and she comes roaring down from the mountain tops – 3,000 odd feet there to roar down into the river miles away, and the big cataract is the only crossing. You've got to cross where there's a bar of rocks as steady as the water and then once she's over, land but the water that's coming down had got a great suction power - you see, coming all the way from the mountains and then it stops at this long water-hole at one place. After that bar of rocks it's just boiling foam as it goes down the mountain, and a poor bloke's grave was there. In my day there was still the wooden cross they chopped from the trees and put it up as a reminder to be bloody careful crossing there... It was terrific that water going down there, if you didn't have horses you had to go on your toes to get across with the swag on your back and horses used to be swept down too - you see.

Charlotte Street, Cooktown when Idriess was there.
Postcard 1910 showing a view of Cooktown.

Charlie Pierce says: "I'll show ya." Well down below the waters did look much calmer lower, that was only because the worst of the fall was just over but there was terrific suction under that still-looking bloody water. He used to think things like that were a joke, but by Christ, I didn't.

The Aboriginal boys used to love him. They used to get him to do this and that they could do naturally and they'd know traps in the ground and soggy water-holes; trying to decoy him when they was out chasing cattle - just to put him in a fix. He'd laugh at them and paddle his way out and he'd say: "I'll never be caught that way again Jacky".

I liked the people so much and they were so variegated. It was such a free life, everyone was everyone's boss in those days. A lot of these people was working forever, they was making their own living - a very happy living. Their own-selves for their own-selves, and that's a wonderful feeling. In those days, to work for a boss you had the sort of democracies we had in the cities - more than anywhere, everytime; the fear of the sack and you had say, ten hours work every day, an hour to work perhaps and an hour to go back with the transport of those days; and you were always scared you or the wife would get sick because that meant you'd be in debt for life.

It was a wonderful feeling to be your own boss, like I always was. It was only in an emergency or if I was nearly broke and particular wanted to be grub-steak then I'd get my own grub-steak...go in for instance, something like a cane-cutting contract. Or working at a shearing shed - that was a very interesting life and I didn't mind the shearing at all. I never got to have the dignity of the shearer of course - not one of the bloody aristocrats of the game but they did at last let me have a learner's spin.

A learner's spin... You know the biggest aristocrats I ever found in my young lifetime was your own fellow workmen, when they got to be a pannikin boss. My flamin' oath, they was the aristocrats of the "silver tails world" in my day, especially those bloody cane-cutting cobbers of mine.

Trooper Ion Idriess of the 5th Light Horse.

20

Life now

I reckon it's wonderful. The only thing that's wrong with it is if anyone gets a chronic sickness though. I reckon doctors should have found the cures for all sicknesses. There have been witch doctors in every race in the world for millions and years and damn me, I've got a bit of corn and they can't even cure that!

Malaria is the only thing that troubles me and that'd be a South American witch doctor who found the cure for that...my oath! I'll give him more credit the old witch doctor.

I'm happy to be living now, although I can only hobble along with a stick and I've got a few old war-wounds - they play up occasionally but not too bad though. Only this damned malaria and then it's this damn wind brings it out. If a certain sort of wind with a chill comes along then I'll know I'm in for it, but I take the quinine here and I'm quite okay.

These days... a bloke couldn't go like Kidman on a one-eyed horse and five bob in his pocket and get to make a hundred stations in his lifetime, and any man could go far out and peg his own land. If he was capable of managing alright, he was set for life of course. But like everything else there's only a certain amount of excellent carpenters, excellent electricians, excellent doctors...my bloody oath! There's only just a percentage of them, of real good doctors like, there's only a certain number of artists - of real good artists and that sort of thing....

I think there's more and more challenges now, and new inventions and new discoveries to find the cure for cancer - for instance, and for many diseases which still cause awful pain and distress and death to people before their time. There's many, many cures....

So many things in commerce to be found out... Just look at the many discoveries - even everyday things, even envelopes, even the cloth that you bind a parcel in shops, they discovered new things for that; well there's big money and everyone wants big money for security, there's big money in everything. You could invent a new sort of bloody fishing line, which they have – anything!

If I were starting adventuring again, I'd learn all I could about electronics, because electronics is only comparatively in the early stage where there is much more to know. I reckon that discoveries can be made, some discoveries have been made where you can walk out the harbour and walk across the sea on some sort of bloody ship... Among the hundreds of thousands of square miles of reef, all those massed vegetation of coral life: God knows what's in them to be found out.

If I could find the inclination I could easily write another 50 books out of those notebooks that I've got over there...easy. And upstairs I've got boxes and boxes the daughter has gone and put away in some place, out of the road somewhere. I've got boxes and boxes of notes. I kept things like that starting from a boy with the *Bulletin* and I'd write things down so you didn't have to trust the memory or think things up. Cripes, I've got enough memories and things in those notebooks to write for a hundred years. I really think especially now... how interesting my life was. I was lucky to be out there...

Australians don't even know things about their own country that was common place in my day. Looking over these notes now and again – I put in a stray hour or two - life was fascinating in those days. Now you can't go out in the bush or look for new rivers or new minerals or things like you could then, and live the islander life. It was wonderful cruising just among our own islands around our coast... You can't now, so you've got to think out something in your mind that's going to interest you - then you're set. Even if it's finding some new flying thing (hang gliding), what the young fellas jumping off this cliff up here and flying without any power...

Now, that's damned interesting and that could be developed a hell of a lot more even than it is. But that'll give you an idea...Who would have thought you could fly in the air (like that) in my day, before Hargreaves and the Wright Bros, and that mob? Look what they've done, they've flown to the bloomin' moon, but who would ever dreamt ten years ago that you'd fly just yourself, make a pair of wings yourself and jump off a cliff and away you buzz.

They look real good. The first one I saw was the other day, went up there and there was these two damned things flying all over the damned place right outside our bloody front lawn.

Oh, I would like to try it and by cripes don't I wish I wasn't toothless, with a broken leg; one leg in the grave and the other halfway there...This arm had been broken five bloomin' times. It's quite okay again now, and those little lumps is from Lone Pine - only tiny pin heads of things but they swell up now and I can't bloody well use it. Tiny pieces of shrapnel, a piece of dirty old shell in there, and I've got a bit in the hips because they didn't dare try and remove them, said: "If we cut that out it's so close to the 'B' artery you're going to bleed to death quick-like".

I said: "Well, leave the bloody thing there!"

Apart from that, life's been good.

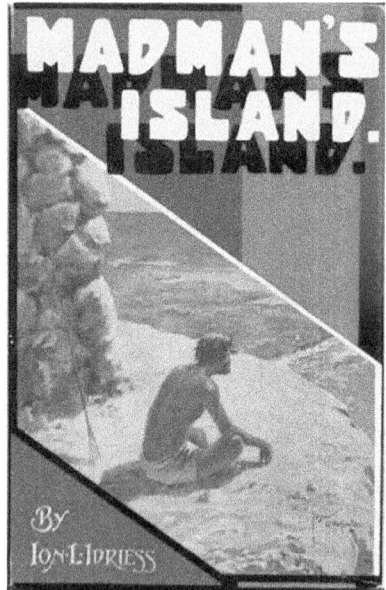

The sniper Billy Sing, whom Idriess would spot for at Gallipoli.
George Robertson, Publisher at Angus & Robertson.
The cover of the 1927 edition of *Madman's Island*.

NOTES

1 - Ion Idriess wrote paragraphs for the Bulletin under the name of Gouger. These stories have been compiled by Jim Bradly, in *Gouger of the Bulletin*, Volumes 1 and 11 (Idriess Enterprises). The full story of Idriess and his time with Tom Peel can be found in the 22nd edition of *Lightning Ridge*, published by ETT Imprint.

2 - The Desert Column was written from his own diaries of his World War One (WW1) campaign as a trooper in the 5th Light Horse, from Gallipoli to Beersheba and beyond. Idriess was prompted to write it as a book by his sister Dycie. It was published in 1932. The 28th edition is published by ETT Imprint, with a new introduction by Ross Coulthart.

3 - Jim Bradly's research into "Gouger", prompted the second volume of *Gouger of the Bulletin*, where can be read Idriess writing as 'Atherton', 'Up Top', 'Up North', 'Ili', 'Three E's', 'Sea-Nomad', 'Fingerpoint' and 'Jack Hall'. Bradly also lists a further 16 possible Idriess pseudonyms in this book, published by ETT Imprint in early 2021.

4 - Madman's Island was first published in April 1927 as an adventure romance. The 1938 edition is written as a true Australian adventure, illustrated by Percy Lindsay. The 9th edition of this version of *Madman's Island* is published by ETT Imprint, with a new introduction by Ernest Hunter.

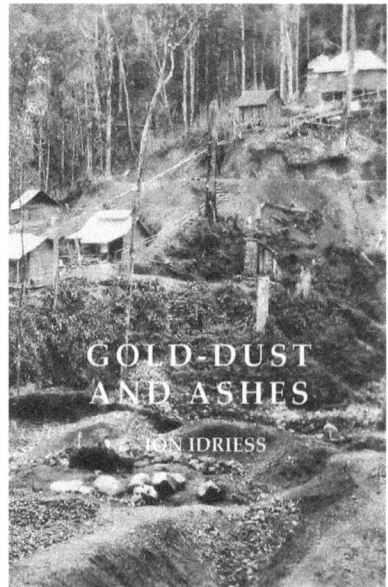

Alec Chisholm teaching bush boys about birds, 1914.
New editions of two Idriess classics.

5 - Alexander Hugh (Alec) Chisholm (1890-1977) spent half his life in the bush researching native birds, the other half as a writer and editor of the Sydney *Daily Telegraph* (from 1922) and the Melbourne *Argus* (1937), and is best-known as editor-in-chief of the ten volume *Australian Encyclopaedia* (1958).

6 - George Robertson (1860-1933) was born in England but came to Australia to try his luck in 1882. Four years later he bought a half-share in a book-selling business with an old colleague, David Mackenzie Angus, and in 1890 the business moved to Castlereagh Street, Sydney. Robertson was principal publisher at Angus & Robertson following Angus's retirement in 1899.

7 - Idriess stayed at 378 Park Road, Paddington, New South Wales, but moved to 5 West Street Paddington in 1929.

8 - *Prospecting for Gold* was first published by Angus & Robertson in February 1931. The 21st edition is available from ETT Imprint.

9 - *Lasseter's Last Ride* was first published by Angus & Robertson in September 1931 and reprinted ten times to December 1932. The 49th edition is available from ETT Imprint.

10 - *My Mate Dick* was written about Richard (Dick) Welsh, whom Idriess knew in WW1. Welsh died of war injuries in 1933. The book was published in 1963, and a new edition will be published in 2021 by ETT Imprint.

11 - The League of Nations gave Australia the mandate to govern the former German colony of New Guinea in May 1921. Gold was discovered in Papua and New Guinea and Idriess wrote the classic history of prospecting there in *Gold-Dust and Ashes*. First published in 1933, the 28th edition of this book is published by ETT Imprint.

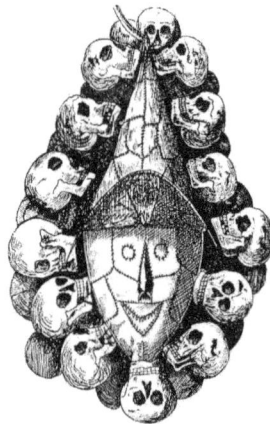

An illustration from *The Shipwrecked Orphans,* showing John Ireland
teaching Duppa to bend iron with fire, following the *Charles Eaton*
shipwreck.
Lower illustrations shows Rev. William Macfarlane, and the Aureed Island
skull trophy, the Au-Gud, as drawn by W.E. Brockett of the *Isabella.*

12 - Idriess was 37 when *Madman's Island* came out but nearing 42 when *Prospecting for Gold* and *Lasseter's Last Ride* were published.

13 - Drums of Mer was first published by Angus and Robertson in September 1933, with an introduction by Reverend William Macfarlane and reprinted four times that year. The 23rd illustrated edition is available from ETT Imprint.

14 - The *Charles Eaton* was a merchant barque built near Madras in 1833. It was wrecked on the Great Barrier Reef near the Sir Charles Hardy Islands. Survivors went on two rafts north and all and all but two were killed by Torres Strait islanders. Only two survived the drama, John Ireland and William D'Oyly, who lived on Mer till 1836. Idriess writes the full story in *Headhunters of the Coral Sea* (ETT Imprint 2021).

15 - The "Charles Eaton tomb", Pioneer Park, Botany Bay Cemetery, Sydney. *The "Charles Eaton" struck rocks near the Sir Charles Hardy Islands on 15 August 1834. She carried a crew of 26, plus seven passen-gers who included Captain and Mrs D'Oyley and their two sons, George and William. Six crew members stole the ship's boats and reached Timor around two months later. The other 27 survivors made two rafts and set out for the mainland where they were captured by aborigines and killed except for George, William and the two cabin boys, John Ireland and William Sexton. George D'Oyley and William Sexton were killed at a later date. Both John Ireland, and the baby, William D'Oyley were saved six years later by a ship searching for survivors (after hearing reports of them).*
45 skulls were found in a hut on Aureed Island. Seventeen of them were European and included Mrs D'Oyley's skull (identified by some of her hair that was still attached). The skulls were taken back to Bunnerong Cemetery for burial. The two boys were located on another island, not Aureed Island which was decimated in retaliation for the deaths.

16 - Reverend William Harold Macfarlane (born 1866) was the Mission priest of Torres Strait and administrator of the Diocese of Carpentaria, and aided Idriess in his research for *Drums of Mer* in 1927. He wrote When Shadows Lengthen: Yarns of Old Identities of the Torres Strait under the name of C. Coral for the *Queenslander,* 3 October 1925.

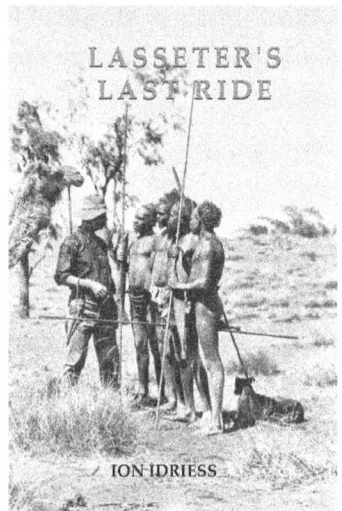

LASSETER'S
LAST RIDE

ION IDRIESS

Bob Buck talking with Aboriginal tribesmen in the desert search for Harold
Lasseter.
Bob Buck, bushman.

17 - Reverend Samuel Macfarlane (1837-1911) was with the London Missionary Society in New Guinea in 1871, Cape York in 1874, then Murray Island (Mer) in 1877. In 1888 he published *Among the Cannibals of New Guinea.*

18 - Edward Vivian Timms (1895-1960) was injured at Gallipoli, and began publishing novels with Angus and Robertson from 1925.

19 - Robert Henry (Bob) Buck (1881-1960) came from a family of Territory pioneers, and was commissioned to find Harold Lasseter in February 1931, found his body and buried it, traveling 1000 miles to pass over evidence to the police. In August 1931 he led a party to find the fabled reef, but the venture was abandoned. His Aranda wife was Molly Tjalameinta.

20 - Kenneth Stuart discovered the Hammerjack Gold Mine at Tennant Creek in 1935, and more than twelve thousand pounds worth of gold out of it. He frittered it away, and was working for wages at nearby Nobles Nob mine when gold was again discovered at Hammerjack in 1949.

21 - Captain Ancell Clement Gregory (1878-1942) arrived in Broome in 1904, and was soon manager of Murphy's fleet of 28 vessels. He was appointed Harbour Master and acquired four schooners. He was President of the Pearler's Association from 1917 to 1923. In 1929 he located ten of his pearling fleet to Darwin, returning to Broome when the Japanese bombed Darwin in 1942.

22 - *Men of the Jungle* was published in 1932, and concerns trekking from Cooktown to Cairns in 1913. He recalled his times with the Aboriginal brothers Norman and Charlie Baird, at China Camp, Bloomfield, and his meeting with the love of his life, Mee-Lele, who had been educated at a Thursday Island convent. The 20th edition will be available from ETT Imprint in 2021.

A steam tram enters Argent Street Broken Hill in 1902.
Idriess's mother Julia.

TIMELINE

1889 - Born at Waverley Sydney, NSW, on 20 September. His father, Walter Owen-Idriess, registered his birth as 'Ion Windeyer' (in reference to his wife Julia Windeyer-Idriess). He took up a position as a sheriff's officer and mines inspector and the family moved to Tenterfield. Idriess always referred to himself as 'Ion Llwellyn Idriess', and simply 'Jack' in the bush.

1893 - The family moved to Lismore.

1895 - Jack was enrolled at Lower Boorie Provisional School.

1897 - The family moved to Tamworth.

1901 - The family moved to Broken Hill.

1905 - Jack won an under 16 essay competition: 'The District We Live In.' Jack left school and worked as a bottle-washer at the Medical Hall Chambers, Argent Street, Broken Hill. Later he worked for White & Hosier, Ore Buyers of Chloride Street.

1907 - In November, Jack contracted typhoid fever and collapsed after his final examination to qualify as an assayer at the Broken Hill School of Mines. He achieved honours in chemistry.

1908 - Jack's mother died of typhoid, contracted while caring for him. The family left Broken Hill for Sydney to live with Jack's grandmother, Mrs Windeyer-Edmunds. In March, Jack ran away to sea on the SS *Newcastle*

First troops out of Townville, on the way to Thursday Island, 1914.
Ion Idriess (left) with his group of 5th Light Horsemen, on the road to Beersheba,
photographed by Barney Haydon.

plying between Sydney and Newcastle and up the Hunter River to Morpeth. Later that year, worked on a station near Narrabri for five months, then spends four months horse-breaking at Moree.

1909 - Jack spent two months with a ring-barking team near Collarenebri, then five months as a rabbit-poisoner on Woorawadian Station, NSW. He spent two months opal mining (gouging) at Lightning Ridge with no luck. This was followed by shearing and shooting dingos and foxes.

1910 - At Lightning Ridge Jack struck opal with Tom Peel and his first article was published in the *Sydney Mail* on July 13. He wrote paragraphs for the *Bulletin's* 'Aboriginalities' page using the pen-name "Gouger."

1911 - Jack's four months droving near Narrabri finished in February. He then worked as a roustabout on Dungeleer Station, NSW before traveling back to Lightning Ridge.

1912 - Jack was blind-stabbing for tin at Slaty Creek, then labouring at Home Rule. He arrived in Cairns in May employed by the Cooktown & Annan River Tin Mining Company with Dick Welsh. He then mined alluvial tin at Rossville, then went hydraulic mining at Mount Finnegan.

1913 - Mined in areas around Cairns and Cooktown, including Mt Frazer, Mareeba, Rossville, Annan River and Herberton.

1914 - Traveled to the top of Cape York Peninsula with Dick Welsh and spent some months with a tribe of Aborigines. Learning of the outbreak of war while prospecting at Cape Melville, he went back to Cooktown, where he took out a Miner's Right on 16 September. He stowed away on the SS *Musgrave* to Cairns. Finding no enlistment post at Cairns, Jack stowed away to Townsville, where he enlisted on 26 October with the 5th Australian Light Horse Regiment.

1915 - Jack landed at Cape Hellas in the Dardanelles from the transport ship *Lutzow* on 18 May. Served in Gallipoli, Sinai and Palestine at the same time as author Arthur Upfield. Jack wrote a daily diary from which *The Desert Column* was written.

Private Norman Baird, an Aboriginal born on the Bloomfield River knew
Idriess in his early Cooktown days, and post-war prospecting.
Marin-Amin men dressed for ceremony at the time of Idriess's visit in 1927.

1918 - Jack was invalided home and discharged on May 10, carrying a number of shrapnel pieces embedded in his body. He spent three months working out at Snowy Baker's Gym in Sydney. By August he had given up his crutches and was with Ildyce in Grafton.

1919 - Jack was in Brisbane in March, then went prospecting around the Daintree and Normanby Rivers with Dick Welsh, Norman and Charlie Baird.

1920 - Arrived on Howick Island in September where he was marooned with another returned soldier-prospector, George Tritton, who tried to kill him. Jack kept a diary in the old log of the *Seafoam*, from which he wrote *Madman's Island*.

1921 - Back in Cooktown in February and goes prospecting with Dick Welsh around the Starcke country.

1922 - Jack stayed with his sister Ildyce in Grafton, writing *Madman's Island* from November to March 1923.

1923 - Jack is reported in the press as giving a blood donation to another war veteran in Brisbane on March 27. He sends the first draft of *Madman's Island* to Alec Chisholm, and George Robertson at Angus & Robertson returns it unread.

1924 - Worked on the Brisbane wharves.

1925 - Jack meets Alec Chisholm and George Robertson in June, while staying at 378 Park Road, Paddington.

1926 - Jack sailed up the Cape York Peninsula in the *Somerset*, in search of gold-bearing country for the Queensland Mines Department. Worked on the Thursday Island wharves and on building the unmanned lighthouse at Restoration Rock.

1927 - Traveled with "The Wandering Missionary", the Reverend Mr Macfarlane on *The Herald*, researching material for *Drums of Mer*. *Madman's Island*, was published in May.

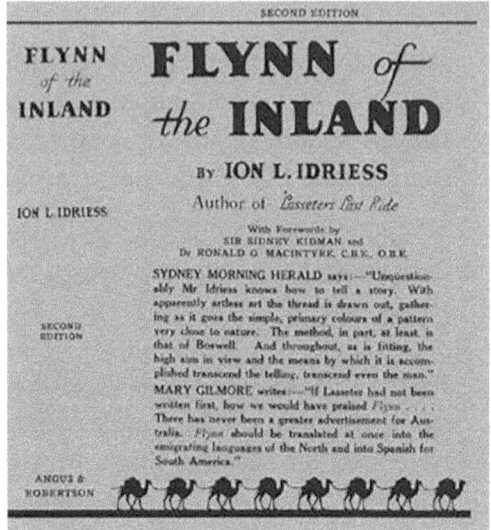

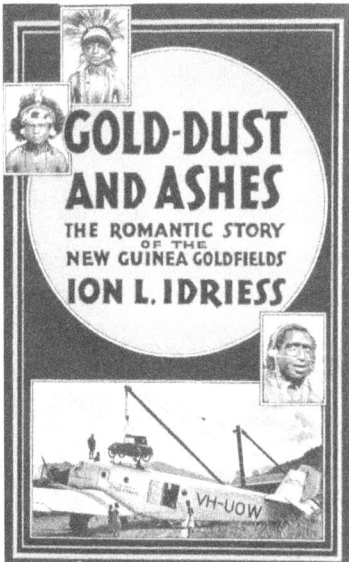

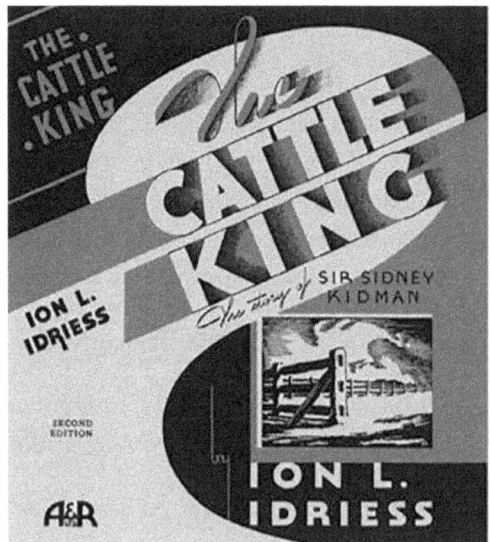

Early editions of Idriess classic tales published by Angus & Robertson.

1928 - Jack sailed to New Guinea, recruiting for pearl divers, and went some way up the Fly River. Later prospecting for gold in north Queensland.

1929 - Returned to Sydney then moved to Grafton with Ildyce to begin work on *The Desert Column*.

1930 - Jack stayed at 5 West Street, Paddington where he wrote *Prospecting for Gold*, then moved to 42 Bayswater Road, Kings Cross.

1931 - *Prospecting for Gold* published in February, reprinting that year. *Lasseter's Last Ride* published in September, reprinting three times that year.

1932 - *Flynn of the Inland* published in March, reprinting five times that year. *The Desert Column* published in April, reprinting three times that year. *Men of the Jungle* published in September, reprint twice that year.

1933 - *Gold-Dust and Ashes* published in April, reprinting four times that year. *Drums of Mer* published in September, reprinting three times that year. A daughter, Judith, is born in February to Jack's companion Eta Gibson.

1934 - Travelled from Sydney to Perth, then extensively throughout Western Australia and into the Northern Territory. Jack spent over two months riding with a Mounted Police Patrol on a mission to bring back to Derby Aboriginal murderers, lepers and any Aboriginals needing medical attention. *The Yellow Joss* and other stories published in June 1934, reprinting that year. Eta Gibson gives birth to a daughter Wendy.

1935 - Returned to South Australia to research the material for *The Cattle King* for the Kidman family. *Man Tracks* was published in March, reprinting six more times that year. Jack lives with Eta and the children at 111 Cottenham Road, Kingsford later that year.

1936 - *Lasseter's Last Ride* was published in England by Jonathan Cape, reprinting that year. *The Cattle King* was published in March, reprinting ten times that year.

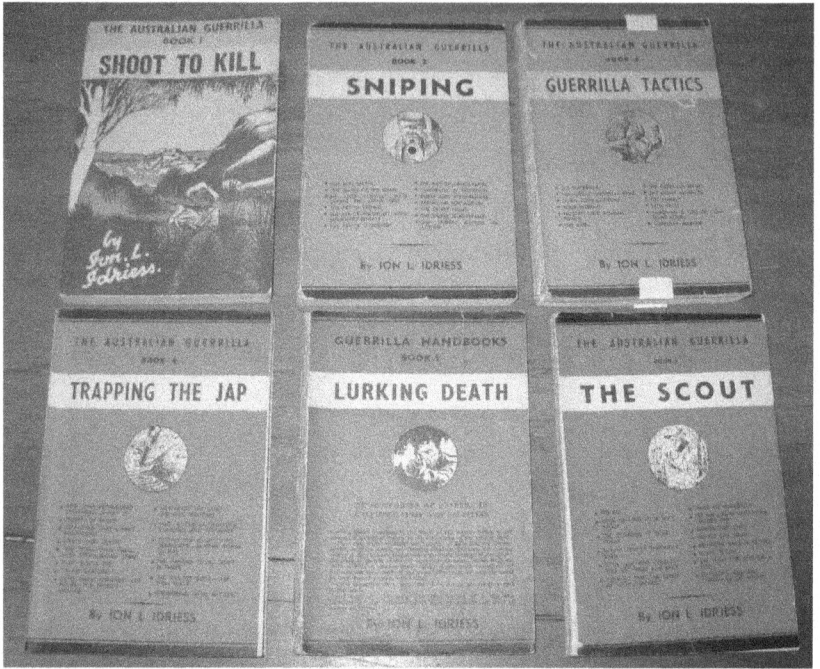

THE AUSTRALIAN GUERRILLA
BOOK I
SHOOT TO KILL
by Ion L. Idriess.

THE AUSTRALIAN GUERRILLA
BOOK 2
SNIPING
By ION L. IDRIESS

THE AUSTRALIAN GUERRILLA
BOOK 3
GUERRILLA TACTICS
By ION L. IDRIESS

THE AUSTRALIAN GUERRILLA
BOOK 4
TRAPPING THE JAP
By ION L. IDRIESS

GUERRILLA HANDBOOKS
BOOK 5
LURKING DEATH
By ION L. IDRIESS

THE AUSTRALIAN GUERRILLA
BOOK 6
THE SCOUT
By ION L. IDRIESS

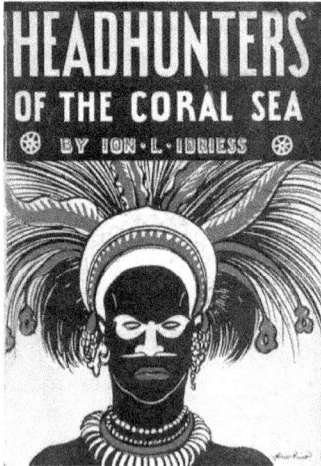

HEADHUNTERS
OF THE CORAL SEA
BY ION·L·IDRIESS

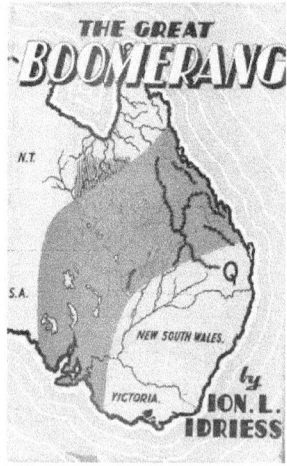

THE GREAT
BOOMERANG
N.T.
S.A.
Q
NEW SOUTH WALES
VICTORIA
by ION. L. IDRIESS

1937 - Jack appeared before the Parliamentary Select Committee Inquiry into Aboriginal Affairs to talk about his experiences and addressed the Agricultural Bureau Conference on soil erosion. Promoted the "Round Australia Motor Contest" as a tourist attraction for the 1938 Sesqui-Centenary. *Forty Fathoms Deep* was published in January, reprinting five times and *Over the Range* published in October, reprinting four times that year.

1939 - In April, Angus & Robertson produced a twelve-volume "National Edition" of Idriess titles: *Flynn of the Inland, Lasseter's Last Ride, Forty Fathoms Deep, The Desert Column, The Cattle King, Gold-Dust and Ashes, Madman's Island, Men of the Jungle, Man Tracks, Over the Range, The Yellow Joss,* and *Drums of Mer. Must Australia Fight?* was published in June and *Cyaniding for Gold* was published in August.

1940 - *Headhunters of the Coral Sea* was published in September. *The Great Trek* was published in October.

1941 - The Australian Army Intelligence Eastern Command asked for an appointment to discuss coast-watching proposal. *Fortunes in Minerals* was published in August. *Nemarluk* was published in October, reprinting that year and *The Great Boomerang* published in December.

1942 - Jack was President of the Defence Auxiliary organization, formed by citizens to defend Australia against invasion by the Japanese. He wrote and A & R published the first five books in 'The Australian Guerrilla Series' handbooks; *Shoot to Kill* and *Sniping* in June, *Guerrilla Tactics* in July, *Trapping the Jap* and *Lurking Death* in September. Jack and family move to Isaac Smith Street, Kingsford.

1943 - Jack's plan for turning the northern rivers inland to the desert caused much controversy. The sixth book in the Guerrilla Series, *The Scout* was published in February.

1944 - *The Silent Service*, written in collaboration with Torpedo-man T. M. Jones was published in March. *Onward Australia* was published in August.

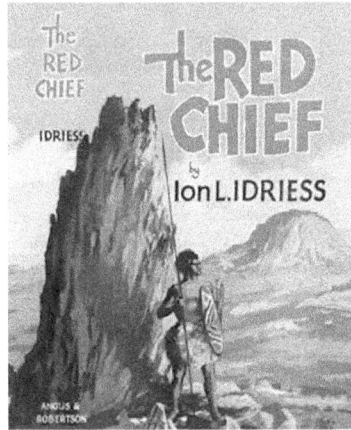

Wendy Idriess (left) with her half-brother Maurice Gibson, and half-sister, Judy Gibson in Sydney 1948. Idriess had a long-term companion, Eta (Morris), who was married to Jesse Gibson. Her son Maurice Beresford Gibson was born in Sydney in 1929. Eta Gibson claims she met idriess in 1932, the same year as the birth of her child Judy. Wendy Eta Idriess was born in 1934. As his biographer Beverley Eley has said, "Jack… accepted full responsibility for Eta and Wendy, the child born while he was traveling in the Kimberley"

1945 - *Horrie the Wog Dog*, written from the diaries of James Bell Moody, was published in June and in the USA by Bobbs-Merrill.

1946 - *In Crocodile Land* published. Eta Gibson begins relationship with Frank Lax.

1947 - *Isles of Despair* published.

1948 - *The Opium Smugglers* published. *Stone of Destiny* published.

1949 - *Gems from Idriess*, a selection for schools, and *One Wet Season* published. Maurice Gibson died at Tennant Creek on 17 August.

1950 - Jack took a trip across the Nullarbor with an Angus & Robertson salesman; he autographed 1200 books in two days at Broken Hill. *The Wild White Man of Badu* published.

1951 - *Across the Nullarbor* published.

1952 - *Outlaws of the Leopolds* published, reprinting that year.

1953 - *The Red Chief* published, reprinting that year.

1954 - *The Nor'-Westers* published.

1955 - *The Vanished People* published.

1956 - *The Silver City* published, reprinting that year.

1957 - Jack is ill with recurring malaria. *Coral Sea Calling* published, reprinting that year.

1958 - *Back O' Cairns* published, reprinting that year. Ill for 59 days of the year with malaria.

1959 - *The Tin Scratchers* published, reprinting that year.

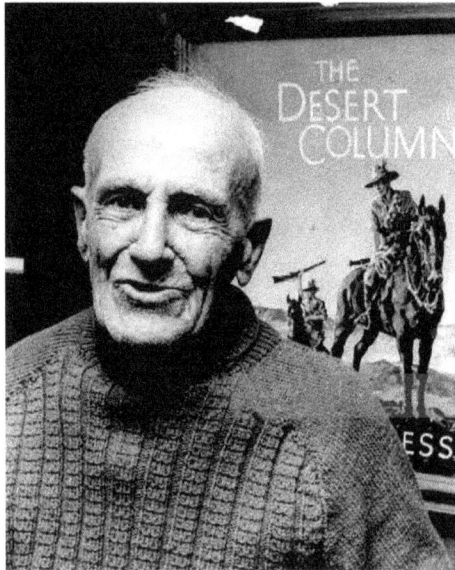

Angus & Robertson authors, from left: Frank Clune, Colin Roderick, E.V. Timms,
Ion Idriess, Colin Simpson and Alec Chisholm.
Idriess at his daughter Wendy's home in Mona Vale, on his 83rd birthday.

1960 - *The Wild North* published.

1961 - *Tracks of Destiny* published.

1962 - *My Mate Dick* published.

1963 - *Our Living Stone Age* published.

1964 - Ill with malaria for 24 days and suffered a stroke; admitted to Concord Repatriation Hospital, Sydney. *Our Stone Age Mystery* published.

1966 - Continued to visit Angus & Robertson every two weeks to autograph books.

1967 - *Opals and Sapphires* published.

1968 - Received an Order of the British Empire for services to publishing.

1969 - *Challenge of the North* published, reprinting that year. *The Diamond* also published that year.

1973 - Best of Idriess series published in hardback by Discovery Press: *The Cattle King, The Desert Column, Drums of Mer, Flynn of the Inland, Forty Fathoms Deep, Lasseter's Last Ride, Lightning Ridge,* and *The Red Chief,*

1975 - Jack's last interview, with Tim Bowden.

1979 - Jack died on 6 June, aged 90. His long-time friend Colin Simpson spoke at his funeral service, while the ode "Age Shall Not Weary Them", was recited by Sir Anthony Trollope, great-great-grandson of the English novelist.

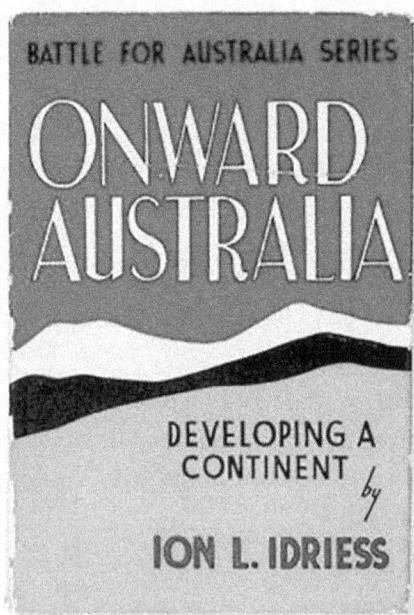

An Idriess photograph from *Man Tracks*; Alec Chisholm with a white-eared honey-eater'; a cartoon of Idriess from the *Bulletin*, 1935.

INDEX

www.ingramcontent.com/pod-product-compliance
Lightning Source LLC
Chambersburg PA
CBHW030944090426
42737CB00007B/533